THE SACRAMENTALS

according to

THE CODE OF CANON LAW

A DISSERTATION

Submitted to the Faculty of Canon Law of the Catholic University of America in partial fulfilment of the requirements for the Degree of Doctor of Canon Law

By the

REV. JOHN LINUS PASCHANG, J. C. L.

of the Diocese of Omaha

WASHINGTON, D. C.

1925

Nihil Obstat:

THOMAS J. SHAHAN,
Censor Deputatus.

Washingtonii, D. C., die 23 Maii, 1925.

Imprimatur:

MICHAEL J. CURLEY,
Archiepiscopus Baltimorensis.

Baltimorae, die 23 Maii, 1925.

TABLE OF CONTENTS

The Sacramentals According to The Code of Canon Law

INTRODUCTION.

The object of the present dissertation is to present a brief study of the *Sacramentals* of the Catholic Church. Written to meet part of the requirements for a degree in the School of Canon Law, the juridical problems involved have naturally received primary attention. Other questions, pertaining to the field of Liturgy, Dogmatic or Moral Theology, have been considered only in as far as solidarity and unity of the study advised. Short historical notes are added for the sake of clarity and intelligibility.

The subject matter itself has been arranged under various headings to allow convenient and logical treatment. Not much effort has been made to deal with any of the *Sacramentals* in particular or in species, as this would evidently pertain more to other branches of the Sacred Sciences. Only the general principles of the law have, as a rule, engaged the writer's attention.

The chapters on exorcism, though not overly pregnant with abstruse juridical principles, have purposely been treated more minutely for pragmatical reasons. For outside the brief treatment contained in current works on Liturgy and Moral Theology, very little literature is at the present time available on this subject.

PART I

CHAPTER I

Etymology of the Word Sacramentum

It is a well-known fact to every student of philology that language has its history as well as nations. Language generally develops and grows with the changes that take place in the civilization of the race that uses the language. New words are constantly coined, old words are forgotten, become obsolete through disuse, or quite frequently undergo such modifications in their use as to convey different ideas to different peoples and succeeding generations.

The merit of this claim can easily be ascertained by taking a brief account of the Latin word *Sacramentum,* as used at the present time in theology. In the Old Latin, the word was used as a well established term of Roman Jurisprudence, and signified a certain "*Cautio*," a warrant or security, consisting of a defined sum of money deposited at the opening of a legal process, and forfeited by the loser.[1] Again it was used for the military oath, which recruits had to take before entering upon service, and by which they swore to be true to the Roman standards, and obedient to their leader.[2]

The religious tone of the word *Sacramentum* when used to denote an *Oath* very probably induced the first Christians to receive the term into their vocabulary to express anything sacred or mysterious. Primitive Christianity no doubt was influenced in this choice by etymo-

1. Varro, *Ling. lat.*, lib. 4.
2. Ramsay, *Manual of Roman Antiquities,* c. IX.—Sohm's, *Institutes of Roman Law,* book II, c. 1.—"*Nam ad eam diem nihil praeter Sacramentum fuerit.*" *Titus Livius,* lib. 22, c. 38.

logically deriving the word from *Sacer, sacrare,* etc. "*Sacramentum* stands for a sacred thing."[3] This distinctive Christian sense of *Sacramentum* appears for the first time in the Old Latin Versions of the Bible, and in the writings of the early Fathers, especially in Tertullian, where it is employed for the Greek word "*Mysterion*" and synonymous with the Latin "*Mysterium.*" It had, in these early times, a very wide range of meaning, including everything religious, sacred and mysterious.[4] The reason why so many meanings were given to the word, is due in good measure to the lack of a well-defined sacramental concept during the first Christian ages. It was only during the course of centuries that the meaning of *Sacramentum* became more precise and was more and more restricted. Apparently St. Augustine was really the first writer who seriously sought to restrict it to a definite class of concepts. Thus he insists that the word shall be used to denote a "sacred sign." "*Signa cum ad res divinas pertinent sacramenta appellantur.*"[5] In one of his sermons he says: "*Ista dicuntur Sacramenta, quia in eis aliud videtur, aliud intellegitur.*"[6] This notion of St. Augustine is retained by all subsequent authors, who define a *Sacramentum* as a "*signum sacrum,*" or "*signum rei sacrae.*" Even St. Thomas writes: "*Sacramentum est in genere signi.*"

During the centuries that followed, a marked tendency to continue the effort of St. Augustine in limiting the use of the word in question is noticeable. In fact, the sacramental concept was rapidly growing clearer and stronger. St. Isidore unfortunately brought the idea of some early writers to the foreground again by insisting

3. A. Réville, *Du sens du mot Sacramentum dans Tertullien.*
4. Cf. Tobias XII, 7; Apoc. XVII, 5; Iraeneus, 1, 2, c. 28, MPG, VII, 804-810.
5. St. Augustine, *epist.* VI, 38, MPL, XXXIII, 527-533.
6. St. Augustine, *serm.* 272, MPL, XXXIII, 527-533.

that the word *Sacramentum* is derived from "*secretum.*" Some writers of the 9th and 10th Century, as Radvert and Ratramnus, followed him.[7] But since the 12th Century the Augustinian formula prevailed: "*Sacramentum sacrum signum est.*" Abelard, for example, says: "*Sacramentum sacrae rei signum.*"[8] Hugh, representing the school of St. Victor, defines a sacrament: "*Sacramentum est corporale vel materiale elementum foris sensibiliter propositum ex similitudine repraesentans, et ex institutione significans, et ex significicatione continens aliquam invisibilem et spiritualem gratiam.*"[9] This definition is indeed an improvement upon St Augustine's in as far as it is more precise and complete. But even it cannot be considered perfect. "Its chief imperfection comes from its not being conceived dependently on the idea of sign."[10] Yet the fundamental notion was correct, so much so, in fact, that at the time of Peter Lombard the word was employed only for such rites as produce or are the cause of grace. The famous definition of Peter Lombard itself: "*Sacramentum enim proprie dicitur quod ita signum est gratiae Dei, et invisibilis gratiae forma, ut ipsius imaginem gerat et causa existat,*" adds little to the given notion, but is of merit in as far as it puts the notion into a suitable form. Hence, subsequent writers adopted the definition of Peter Lombard. Even the Council of Trent, found no change necessary.[11] Theologians following the Council of Trent have, however, formulated the definition of a Sacrament in different words, to be in perfect accord with the teachings of the famous Council. As for example, Suarez, whose definition is widely recognized and commonly used: "*Sacramentum est signum sensibile,*

---

7. Pourrat, *Theology of the Sacraments*, p. 36.
8. Abelard, *Intro. ad Theo.*, lib. 1, c. 2, MPL, CLXXVI, 985.
9. Hugh of St. Victor, lib. 1, MPL, CLXXVI, 316.
10. Pourrat, *Theology of the Sacraments*, p. 40.
11. *Conc. Trident.*, sess. VII, *de sacramentis in genere.*

ad sanctitatem aliquam conferendam et veram animae sanctitatem significandam institutum."[12]

From these references and quotation, which might indeed be multiplied indefinitely, the conclusion may, in the opinion of the writer, be legitimately drawn, that the notion of the first Christian Ages, regarding what now in technical theology are called the Sacraments, was very hazy. And it is precisely for this reason, because of this hazy notion of former times, that it seemed good to dwell upon this primitive concept of a Sacrament to an extent that might at first seem somewhat out of proportion by reason of the nature of the matter that is to follow. Yet it must be borne in mind, that before the twelfth century the term *Sacramentum* was so comprehensive as to include "all sacred usages and ceremonies, even such as were not sacramental rites in the technical sense."[13] Quite naturally the *Sacramenta* of these ages were therefore numerous and diversified. They included not merely the seven Sacraments as we have them now, but many other pious objects, sacred rites, prayers, and especially what in modern language are known as the "SACRAMENTALS."[14] Evidently the clear distinction between the Sacraments proper and these pious rites, ceremonies, objects, etc., could not be drawn until a sound and correct definition of "*Sacramentum*" had been reached, and hence it is that before the twelfth and thirteenth century Sacraments and Sacramentals were alike included in the term "*Sacramenta*."[15] This fact, however, would not justify the opinion that no distinction was made regarding the importance and efficacy of these *Sacramenta*. Even the first Christians looked upon some

---

12. Suarez, *Opera Omnia*, vol. XX, quest. LX, disp. I, sect. IV, n. 3.
13. Pohle-Preuss, *Sacraments*, I, c. 2.
14. "*Praeter Sacramenta proprie dicta, alias quoque res sacras habet Ecclesia, quae olim latiori quidem ac minus proprio sensu etiam Sacramenta vocabantur. A multis autem saeculis in morem venit ut Sacramentalia appellentur.*" Conc. Plen. Balt. II, n. 341.
15. Wernz, *Jus Decretalium*, III, n. 758.

of the "*Sacramenta*" as more important, necessary and of greater efficacy than others. During the Middle Ages the "*Sacramenta*" were divided into two classes, the "*Sacramenta,*" properly so called (at times also called *Sacramenta Principalia*), and the *Sacramenta minora*. Hugh of St. Victor (1097-1141) writes: "*Sacramenta minora in quibus etsi principaliter salus non constet, tamen salus ex iis augetur, in quantum devotio exercetur.*"[16] The word "*Sacramentalia*" itself was coined by Alexander of Hales (1245).[17] St. Thomas refers to them in two different expressions, namely: "*Sacra*" and "*Sacramentalia.*"[18] But the distinction was especially marked by the Council of Trent.[19]

---

16. Hugh of St. Victor, *De Sacramentis*, II, 9, MPL, CLXXVI, 471.
17. Augustine, *Commentary on Canon Law*, IV, 558.
18. Pohle-Preuss, *Sacraments*, I, 113.
19. *Conc. Trident.*, sess. VII, *de sacramentis in genere.*

CHAPTER II

A. Notion and Division of Sacramentals

Etymologically considered, *Sacramental* refers to anything that pertains to a Sacrament, especially to the ceremonies and things accidental to the Sacraments: "*Hi ritus quos in Sacramentorum administratione ecclesia observat, vocantur 'Sacramentalia' i. e. res pertinentes ad Sacramenta.*"[1] This notion of ceremonies, was attached to the word by practically all writers up to the time of Suarez. In recent centuries some efforts have indeed been made to restrict the use of the word to certain sacred rites imitative of the Sacraments, and thereby exclude such ceremonies and rites as were merely accidental to the Sacred Services and the administration of the Sacraments.[2] Still these efforts were not of an authoritative nature. The results were theoretical rather than practical and ended in this, that very few writers or students of the subject agreed in the notion or definition of a Sacramental.[3] Hence it is, that almost every writer surprises us with a notion that is frequently and in many respects unique.[4] No wonder, then, that Dr. Schmid could enumerate as many as twelve different definitions of theologians prominent in the field of the Sacraments and Sacramentals.[5] Pesch, for example, defines the Sacramentals in the following words: "*Sacramentalia sunt vel caerimoniae sacrae ab ecclesia institutae vel res ab ecclesia ad pium fidelium usum*

1. Pesch, *Prael. Dog.*, vol. VI, n. 328.—Pohle-Preuss, Sacr. vol. I, p. 113.
2. Lambing, *Sacramentals of the Cath. Church,* c. 1.—Pohle-Preuss, *Sacraments,* vol. I, c. 2.
3. Wernz, *Jus Dec.* III, n. 758 (in footnote).
4. Lambing, *op. cit.,* c. 1.
5. Dr. Schmid, *Die Sakramentalien der Kath. Kirche,* n. 16.

benedictae."[6] Arendt's definition is somewhat longer: "*Signa ad cultum Dei externum legitime instituta, quibus Ecclesia Christi tanquam instrumentis utitur ad ceteros effectus supernaturales in sua ordinaria potestate contentos, praeter proprium sacramentorum propriumque Sacrificii effectum, fidelibus impertiendos.*"[7]

Without questioning the merit of these various definitions, it will be more to our purpose to adhere to the notion set down by the Code of Canon Law, in canon 1144: "*Sacramentalia sunt res aut actiones quibus Ecclesia, in aliquam Sacramentorum imitationem, uti solet, ad obtinendos, ex sua impetratione, effectus praesertim spirituales.*"

B. *Division*

The liberal number of definitions used in pre-Code days quite naturally led also to a marked discrepancy among authors concerning the divisions of the Sacramentals. Many writers felt contented at quoting the divisions expressed in the time-honored hexameter: "*Orans, tinctus, edens, confessus, dans, benedicens.*"[8]

Orans: referred to prayers, especially the Lord's Prayer.

Tinctus: applied chiefly to the use of Holy Water, Consecrated Oils, etc.

Edens: The eating of blessed things, chiefly blessed bread.

Confessus: acts of external humiliations, and the general avowal of our sinfulness and imperfections.

Dans: signified Almsgiving.

Benedicens: blessings and consecrations.

---

6. Pesch, *op. cit.*, vol. VI, sect. 7.
7. Arendt, *De Sacramentalibus*, p. 7. St. Alphonsus, 1, VI, tract. I, c. 4.
8. St. Alphonsus 1. cit.

Others again used the sevenfold divisions contained in the following line: "*Crux, aqua, nomen, edens, ugens, jurans, benedicens.*"

However, when applied to canon 1144 of the Code, it is to be feared that this classification is of little weight and scientific value. For, as will appear later, the prescriptions of the Code are hardly kind enough to embrace these various classes of pious acts in the category of Sacramentals.[9]

A division somewhat more to the point might be made:

1. *Ratione Institutoris*:
   a) Some Sacramentals are determined by Christ immediately, as for example the Washing of Feet.
   b) Others are determined by Christ only mediately, in as far as He gave the Church the power of instituting them. For example, the various benedictions.

2. *Ratione Objecti*:
   a) *Res*: when the spiritual effect is produced through the means of blessed objects, *e. g.*, Holy Water.
   b) *Actiones*: when the effect is produced immediately, as in the case of blessings. These are known also by the name of Transient Sacramentals, because of the passing quality of the act of blessing. Whereas the *Res*, are at times called Permanent Sacramentals because of their lasting nature.

---

9. Pohle-Preuss, 1. cit.

3. *Ratione Ministri*:
   a) Sacramentals whose administration is reserved to a special minister or special Order.
   b) Sacramentals whose administration is not thusly reserved, as specified in canons 1146 and 1147.

4. *Ratione Formae*:
   a) Some require a prescribed form *ad validitatem.*
   b) Others do not require such a form *ad validitatem* (Can. 1148, §2).

5. Some writers make a further distinction into:
   a) Sacramentals that can be repeated.
   b) Sacramentals that cannot be repeated.[10]

Suarez and Bellarimine carry these distinctions still farther, in consequence of the fact that they look upon certain ceremonies as Sacramentals, which according to present-day theologians cannot share that privilege. Yet they had a legitimate reason for instituting their partitions, as Arendt well asserts: *"Eximius recte potuit hujusmodi instituere partitionem, quippe qui de caeremoniis sacramentorum praesertim tractans contra hereticos, eas etiam complexus est et divisit quae solum in significando consistunt.*[11]

---

10. St. Thomas, p. III, Q. 86 & Q. 82, 8 ad 2.
11. Arendt, *op. cit.* p. 17.

CHAPTER III

Sacraments and Sacramentals Compared

Article I. Similarity

The Sacramentals as well as the Sacraments belong to the class of external, sensible signs of religion. What Bellarmine says with respect to a Sacrament may quite properly be applied also to the Sacramentals: "*Sacramentum enim intrinsice et essentialiter est Caeremonia religionis; caeremonia autem est actus externus.*"[1] Ceremony is here used by Bellarmine in the wide sense, including all external acts of worship. Some of these external acts of worship, as is well known, were instituted by Christ; others by the Church. One class, the Sacraments, was instituted for the justification of man; another class, the Sacramentals, was destined to produce certain effects, spiritual and temporal, outside the justification of man, and a third class, ceremonies in the strict sense, was intended to add to the solemnity of Divine Cult, and the administration of the Sacraments.[2] The Code calls due attention to this external, or sensible characteristic of the Sacramentals, by calling them *res aut actiones.* "*Res,*" includes blessed or consecrated objects, as for example, candles, chalices, etc. The "*actiones*" are divided into consecrations, benedictions and exorcisms. These "*res aut actiones*" are, however, not merely sensible signs, but also *sacred signs,* inasmuch as they are used to obtain a spiritual or supernatural effect. "There must always be a proper relation between the sign and the thing signified, wherefore, if the thing

1. Bellarmine, *Opera Omnia,* Tomus III, lib. I, p. 30.
2. Katschthaler, *Theo. Dog.,* vol. IV, n. 164.

signified be of a spiritual or supernatural order, the sign itself must be sacred. If the Sacraments did not possess some kind of resemblance to the things which they signify, they would not be Sacraments."[3] Noldin calls these signs, therefore, "*signa practica,*" because they not only signify the spiritual effects, but really produce the spiritual result, although not in the same manner, nor in the same degree as the Sacraments. "*Sacramentalia sunt signa practica, quae effectus non solum significant, sed etiam producunt.*"[4] Vermeersch likewise points out the practicalness of these sacred signs, when he remarks: "*Sacramenta enim sunt res vel observationes sacrae, operantes gratiam quam significant.*"[5]

The similarity between the Sacramentals and the Sacraments demanded by the Code, "*in aliquam Sacramentorum imitationem,*" lies, therefore, chiefly in this, that the former as well as the latter consist of visible signs—matter and form—producing a supernatural effect.[6] These very characteristics distinguish the Sacramentals from mere ceremonies as well as the Sacraments. Formerly theologians classed all ceremonies as Sacramentals, forgetting that most of the ceremonies used by the Church are merely symbolical and do not produce a supernatural effect. "*Hae res vocantur Sacramentalia tum quia quandam cum sacramentis similitudinem prae se ferunt, tum ut hoc nomine ab ipsis sacramentis distinguantur.*"[7] Hence, the Sacramentals resemble the Sacraments in as far as the essential requisites are concerned, namely, the sensible sign, producing the spiritual effect.[8]

---

3. St. Augustine, Ep. 98, 9. MPL, XXXIII, 364.
4. Noldin, *Summa Theo. Moralis,* vol. III, n. 44.
5. Vermeersch-Creusen, *Epitome Juris Canonici,* vol. II, n. 462.
6. Pohle-Preuss, *Sacraments,* c. 2.
7. Pesch, *op. cit.,* vol. VI, n. 332.
8. Cappello, *De Sacramentis,* vol. I, n. 99.

Article II. Differences

The difference between the Sacraments and the Sacramentals is chiefly threefold, namely:

1) *Ratione originis.*

2) *Ratione effectus.*

3) *Ratione modi operandi.*[9]

Each of these differences deserves a somewhat detailed consideration.

1. Difference, *ratione originis*

All the Sacraments were instituted by Christ, and by Christ alone. This is *de Fide*: *"Si quis dixerit, Sacramenta novae legis non fuisse omnia a Jesu Christo Domino nostro instituta . . . anathema sit."*[10] This Divine institution is essential to a Sacrament. The Sacramentals need not, however, be of Divine origin.[11] Canon 1145 clearly indicates this: *"Nova Sacramentalia constituere aut recepta authentice interpretari, ex eisdem aliqua abolere aut mutare, sola potest Sedes Apostolica."*

This canon is a response to the frequent objection raised by heretics of all times against the right of the Church to institute and constitute sacred Rites, Ceremonies and Sacramentals. From the very first Christian Ages, we find enemies of the Christian Religion condemning external acts of religion as foolish and superstitious.[12] They charged the Church with reinstating the ceremonies of the Old Jewish Religion,[13] the laws of the Old Covenant, and then launched against her the text of St. Paul: "Behold, I, Paul, tell you that if you be circumcised Christ shall profit you nothing."[14]

---

9. Noldin, *op. cit.* l. cit.
10. Conc. Trent, *Sess. VII, de sac. in gen.*, *Denz-Bann.*, n. 844.
11. Lambing, *op. cit.*, c. 1.
12. Cocaleo, *Tentamina Theo.—Mor. Tom. III, disc. III*, c. 3.
13. Pohle-Preuss, l. cit.
14. Gal. V, 2.

Or again, it is maintained that these rites were copied from pagan superstitions, and hence offensive to the God of the Christians, and superstitious. According to another class, the right of changing rites and ceremonies cannot be reserved by the Church, since the Christian Religion is not a religion of serfdom, but a religion of freedom, in which the *lex libertatis* is supreme. They maintain that every individual has the right to use or omit or change ceremonies, as he sees fit. As a support for their notion they resort to St. Augustine's letter to Januarius, where he writes: "*. . . . habere liberas observationes.*" They furthermore insist that Christ did not desire to encumber Christian worship with many and detailed Rites and Ceremonies, since He Himself instituted but so few Sacraments, and legislated very little concerning external worship.[15] The canon is against another class of heretics who charged the Church with contempt for the Rites and Ceremonies introduced by the Apostles and left to them by Christ. For example, the potion of milk and honey administered during early centuries to those that were baptized, has been abolished.[16] They argue that if the Church sees fit to abolish these ceremonies, it should also abolish others, as for example, exorcism, anointings, etc. A similar opinion is fostered by others, when they grant the Church the right of changing ceremonies, etc., but deny unto her the exclusive right. According to them, the rites and ceremonies used by the Church were introduced, not by any special legislation, but rather by custom and practice of the faithful. Hence, if they owe their origin to the faithful, these same faithful should be allowed to change or abolish the Old Rites and introduce new ones.[17]

---

15. Suarez, *Opera Omnia,* vol. XX, Quest. LXV, Disp. XV, sect. 2. Berti, *Opus de Theo. Discip.*, lib. XXX, c. 30.
16. Tertullian, *de coron.* c. III, MPL, II, 79.—Barnab. ep. c. VI, MPG, II, 739.—Probst, *Sakramente u. Sakramentalien,* p. 151.
17. Berti, *op. cit.* lib. XXX, c. 22.

Now, the errors of the early heretics were espoused in some shape or another by the advocates of the Reformation. Wycliff, for example, denied that any effects were conferred by the Rites and Sacramentals. Blessings, according to his opinion, were vain and foolish. Luther advocated a belief in the sign of the cross and exorcism, but regarded all other rites as *ad libitum,* and merely empty symbols devoid of any effect, especially spiritual. Still, he never denied the Church the right of instituting them. The Waldenses ridiculed all blessings performed by the Church.[18] Calvin speaks in a rather harsh and irreligious manner of the Rites and Ceremonies of the Church: *"Quasi res esset contemptibilis ex Christi praecepto aqua baptizare, inventa est benedictio vel potius incantatio quae veram aquae consecrationem pollueret. Additus postea cereus cum chrismate, exsufflatio vero januam ad Baptismum aperire visa est. Etsi autem me non latet, quam vetusta sit adventitia huius farraginis origo, respuere tamen mihi et piis omnibus fas est, quidquid ad Christi institutionem addere ausi sunt homines . . . . Cum autem videret Satan stulta mundi credulitate absque negotio fere inter ipsa Evangelii exordia receptas esse suas imposturas, ad crassiora ludibrio prorupit."*[18a] Melanchthon maintained that the Church could institute rites and ceremonies for the instruction and edification of the faithful, but without any effect.[19]

In noting these heretical opinions it will have been observed that the words "Rites" and "Ceremonies" are used instead of "Sacramentals." The reason for this lack of distinction is as has been pointed out previously, that the word "Sacramentals" was not, until comparatively recent times, of universal usage. At the

18. cf. Katschthaler, *Theo. Dog.* vol. IV, n. 164.
18a. Calvin, *Instit.* l. 4, c. 15.—cf. Katschthaler, l. cit.
19. Knoll, *Instit. Theo. Theore.* pars. IV, sec. 2, art. 9. Suarez, l. cit. Berti, op. & l. cit.

time when the heretics spoken of, raised their objections against the practices of the Church, the term "Ceremony" and "Rite" comprised not merely ceremonies strictly so called, but rather all exterior worship outside the Sacraments, including, therefore, all sacramentals. In fact, it would have been quite impossible for these objectors to observe, in their remonstrances, an accurate distinction between mere ceremonies, *"in sensu stricto,"* and Sacramentals, as now understood in technical theology, since the basis of the distinction, namely: the special efficacy which the Church ascribes to the latter, by reason of her impetrations, would have quite exceeded the range of their religious conceptions. Hence, when it is urged that the Church has no power to institute ceremonies, the challenge applies to the Sacramentals as well. If the ceremonies of the Church as spoken of by them are foolish, wrong and superstitious, it follows that the Sacramentals must meet the same condemnation; because in all these above stated notions the word "Ceremonies" or "Rites" is used in a *wide* sense.

Canon 1145 clearly defines the jurisdiction which the Church claims in the matter of the Sacramentals. In bygone centuries she has zealously defended her external worship and so she will continue for time to come.[20] The objectors of the above named classes evidently forget that man is a being composed of body and soul, that is, of the material and spiritual, substances that are highly dependent one on the other. The activities, the operations, the movements of the human soul are materially influenced by external experiences.[21] The Church has ever been mindful of this fact. Christ Himself, understanding perfectly the relations of the material and spiritual in

---

20. *Acta et Decreta Conc. Pl. Balt. II,* n. 344: *"Aquae lustralis seu benedictae usus a primis Ecclesiae temporibus repetendus est. Antiqui etiam Sacramenti haud proprie dicti nomine saepe cohonestabant . . ."*

21. Bellarmine, l. cit.

man, ever so often, in His teachings and works, availed Himself of the effects brought about by this union. He, in restoring the sight to the blind man, employs a paste. He imposes hands on the children when blessing them.

Following the footsteps and the example set down by her Divine Founder, the Church at all times has aimed at edifying her children, exciting them unto devotion, by having recourse to external worship.[22] The underlying motive is keenly betrayed by the Council of Trent: "*Cumque natura hominum ea sit, ut non facile queat sine adminiculis exterioribus ad rerum divinarum meditationem sustolli, propterea pia mater Ecclesia ritus quosdam, ut scilicet quaedam submissa voce, alia vero elatiore in Missa pronuntiarentur instituit, ceremonias item adhibuit, ut mysticas benedictiones, lumina, thymiamata, vestes aliaque id genus multa ex Apostolica disciplina et traditione quo et maiestas tanti sacrificii commendaretur, et mentes fidelium per haec visibilia religionis et pietatis signa ad rerum altissimarum quae in hoc sacrificio latent contemplationem excitarentur.*"[23] But not content with merely edifying the faithful and leading them unto devotion, the Church has attached to certain rites and devotions a special efficacy.[24] To some she has attached indulgences, others again she has raised to the rank of Sacramentals, which are destined to produce an extraordinary effect, both temporal and spiritual, by virtue of her sustaining prayer to Almighty God, in behalf of those who properly use or receive them." "*Ad obtinendos ex sua impetratione effectus praesertim spirituales.*"[25] The power of this ordination, the power of creating Sacramentals, the Church vindicates unto herself in the canon cited. And although the wording

22. Cocaleo, l. c.
23. *Conc. Trent. sess. XXII de Sacrificio Missae*, c. 5, Denz-Bann. 943. Pohle-Preuss, *op cit.*, vol. I, p. 112.
24. Pohle-Preuss, l. cit.
25. Canon 1144.

of the canon is new in itself, the power has existed at all times and has been exercised by her at all times.[26] Restricting the term "Sacramental" to the scope properly indicated in the division, "*ratione objecti,*" namely: blessings, consecrations and exorcisms, we can have no doubt that all these three classes of Sacramentals existed already in apostolic times and have endured through these nineteen centuries.

That the power of constituting Sacramentals, which the Church claims in canon 1145 is reasonable and legitimate, is a matter that can hardly be called into question.[27] It is a power which Christ conferred upon her in the plainest terms. He gave the Apostles and the Church the power over unclean spirits: "Heal the sick, raise the dead, cleanse the lepers, cast out devils, freely have you received, freely give."[28] He gives them the example: "And when He had commanded the multitude to sit down upon the grass He took the five loaves and two fishes, and looking up to heaven he blessed and brake . . ."[29] They were commanded to anoint the sick: "And they cast out many devils and anointed with oil many that were sick and healed them."[30] These rites, as exercised by the Apostles before the Ascension, were, however, not Sacramentals in the strict sense of the term. They lacked the supporting prayer of the Church, which, as shall be shown later, is an essential characteristic. Their wonderful effect was due to certain "*charismata,*" given to them by Christ for evident reasons.[31] After the establishment of Christianity these observances were adopted into the Church, not as mere ceremonies, but rather as imitations

26. Wernz, *Jus Dec. Tom. III*, n. 758.
27. Pohle-Preuss, *op cit.* pp. 115-116.
28. Matt. X, 8.
29. Matt. XIV, 19.
30. Mark, VI, 13.
31. Noldin, *op. cit.* vol. III, n. 50.

of the Sacraments, productive of an effect by reason of the Church's prayer. Thus exorcism was made use of by the Apostles even after the Ascension of Christ. It was very common in the early Church and was extended from the exorcism pronounced over human being to the exorcism of inanimate objects, *e. g.*, exorcism of the Baptismal Water.[32] Various kinds of blessings were introduced: *"Ungi quoque necesse est eum qui baptizatus sit, ut accepto Chrismate, id est, unctione, esse unctus Dei et habere in se gratiam Dei possit. Porro autem Eucharistia et unde baptizati unguntur, oleum in altari sanctificatur."*[33] In truth, the claim of St. Paul is quite in place: "Let a man so account of us as of the ministers of Christ, and the dispensers of the mysteries of God."[34] The power of attaching a special efficacy to these blessings, consecrations and exorcisms, is surely not out of keeping with the ultimate end of the Church, nor is the exercise of this power in excess of her faculties. "All power is given to me in Heaven and on earth."[35] And again: "Feed my lambs, feed my sheep."[36] In as far, therefore, as these sacramentals serve as acts of the purest worship and are exceedingly beneficial to man, they may be legitimately established by the Church and supported by her special intercession.[37]

Conscious of this Divine Commission, the Church has, since Apostolic times, made use of Sacramentals. She has received new ones and modified those that she had, so that now there are ever so many benedictions, various classes of consecrations, various kinds of exorcism. And yet the Church's ordination regarding the Sacramentals is not an arbitrary or rather unprin-

---

32. Entychian, *Exhortatio*, MPL, V, 168.
33. Cyprian, Ep. 70, MPL, IV, 408.
34. I. Cor. IV, 1.
35. Matt. XXVIII, 18.
36. John XXI, 16 & 17.
37. Suarez, vol. XX, quest. LXV, disp. XV, sect. 3, n. 3. Pohle-Pruess, *op. cit.*, p. 116.

cipled administration. The Sacramental affairs are under the special supervision of the Holy See. Formerly, during early Christian times, the Apostolic See did not exercise the same vigilance, as regards the Sacramental affairs, as today, which fact will receive attention in a subsequent chapter. But today the Holy See alone can institute new blessings or consecrations or exorcisms. "This is not surprising," writes Fr. Augustine, "if we remember the general saying: *lex orandi lex credendi*. The Sacramentals are the living expression of the faith and hope that is in the Church."[38] Furthermore, the canon reserves to the Holy See the *exclusive* right of interpreting the Sacramentals authoritatively, that is, as to their effect, or nature or signification, as well as to the condition of their administration.[39] This, of course, does not mean that the Sacramentals are of *purely* ecclesiastical origin. Their institution by the Church is a response to the special power which Christ left to His Church.[40] Likewise must the notion be abandoned that these Sacramentals work independently of the good pleasure of the Most High. God alone can attach a spiritual effect to a sensible sign, and every spiritual effect must, after all, come from Him, so that, without the divine will, the blessings of the Church would be ineffectual.[41] God is and remains the *causa efficiens*. Nor is it lawful for us to hold that, by virtue of this canon, all the Sacramentals were officially instituted by the Holy See. In the primitive Church, especially during the apostolic times, rites and ceremonies arose in great numbers and species, which the Holy See did not and could not expressly approve, because of the conditions and imperfect administration of the Church at that time. The Canon is fully cognizant of this fact, and amply

---

38. Augustine, *op. cit.*, vol. IV, p. 559.
39. Vermeersch-Creusen, *op. cit.*, vol. II, n. 464.
40. Bellarmine, *Opera Omnia, Tom.* III, lib. II, pp. 140-145.
41. Vermeersch-Creusen, *Epit. J. Canonici*, vol. II, n. 464.

provides by stating that now and for time to come, the Apostolic See alone has the power to interpret these Sacramentals now in use. "This does not mean that no Sacramentals were instituted without the concurrence of the Apostolic See. For more than one of them, especially the rites surrounding the administration of Baptism, are undoubtedly of Apostolic origin."[42]

The Church can also suppress the Sacramentals. This follows from the fact that she has the power of instituting them. For the former implies the latter. "*Omnis res, per quascunque causas nascitur per easdem dissolvitur.*"[43] The canon insists, however, "*ex eisdem aliqua abolere.*" Absolutely speaking, the Church could of course abolish all the Sacramentals. She received them, constituted or instituted them, and hence can also abolish them. Practically considered, however, she cannot quash them all. Such a course would be prejudicial to the end for which she was instituted. These Sacramentals were established for the purpose of Divine Cult, and the benefit, temporal as well as spiritual, of the faithful, for which reason it is evident that their suppression would result in a detraction from Divine Cult,[44] and entail a loss to the faithful. "*Non omnia simul, utpote ecclesiae valde utilia.*"[45] The question is theoretical, however, rather than practical: "*Verum nullo pacto permitti valeat, venerabiles adeo Ritus ac traditum a Patribus, sancteque ab Ecclesia servatum huiusmodi Sacramentalium usum penitus aboleri.*"[46]

This right of suppressing Sacramentals, as stated above, belongs exclusively to the Holy See. The term Holy See must be understood in the light of canon seven

42. Augustine, *op. cit.*, vol. IV, p. 560.
43. Reg. Juris, 35 in VI°.—*Cf. Blat, De Sacramentis*, lib. III, p. 720.
44. Cocalco, *op. cit.*, Tom. III, Disc. III, c. 3.
45. Blat, *Comment. Text. J. Canonici*, vol. III, p. 720.
46. Benedictus XIV, const. "*Omnium Sollicitudinum,*" 12 Sept. 1744, No. 32, Fontes, n. 348.

of the Code,[47] including, therefore, the Sacred Congregation of Rites. The reason of this provision is quite apparent. The Sacramentals being next to the Sacraments the most effectual fountains of grace and blessing, should not be despised, that is to say, in any way maltreated. "*Si quis dixerit, receptos et approbatos Ecclesiae Catholicae ritus, in solemni sacramentorum administratione adhiberi consuetos aut contemni aut sine peccato a ministris pro libito amitti aut in novos alios per quemcunque ecclesiarum pastorem mutari posse A. S.*"[48] The argument is of course not direct or positive, but sufficient for the present need. For it must again be remembered that the term "ceremonies" or "rites," as used by the Council, did not exclude Sacramentals. If the Church is so jealous about maintaining *all* the rites and ceremonies she uses in the administration of the Sacraments, free from corruption, and anathematizing those that would sanction their contempt, or would permit ministers to omit or change them, it may be legitimately argued that she would *a fortiori* safeguard from every taint of corruption, especially those rites which she has raised to the dignity of Sacramentals. The canon of the Tridentine Council is comprehensive. No rites are excluded. Since then all three classes of Sacramentals, namely Benedictions, Consecrations and Exorcisms, are represented in the administration of the various Sacraments, it follows that these, according to the teaching of the Council, cannot be changed or omitted or despised without incurring the censure of the Council. The Profession of Faith formulated by this same Council is no less insistent, in its prescriptions: "*Receptos quoque et approbatos Ecclesiae Catholicae ritus in supradictorum omnium Sacramentorum sollemni adminisatione*

47. Blat. *op. cit.*, vol. III, pp. 720-721.

48. Conc. Trident. sess. VII, *de Sacramentis in genere,* can. 13.

recipio et admitto."[49] It follows, therefore, that these Sacramentals must be treated with, and held in, sacred reverence.[50] Wherefore the attitude whereby the Church so jealously adheres to these rites and "consistently refuses to depart from such practices as anointings, spittle, breathing, even among nations who were opposed to these rites."[51]

A response given by the Sacred Congregation of the Propagation of the Faith to the Missionaries of China sums up the attitude of the Church regarding the abolition or change of the Sacramentals in unmistakable terms. It was asked whether the missionaries might desist, in the administration of Baptism, from the anointing with the oil of catechumens, or the administration of salt and the anointing with spittle, when such Baptism was to be given to women, "*quia chinenses, magno zelo ducuntur erga uxores, filias et alias mulieres et scandalum sument ex huiusmodi actionibus.*" The reply read thusly: "*Censuerunt, et Sacramentalia in Baptismo mulierum esse adhibenda* (*et Extremam Unctionem esse mulieribus conferendam*); *nec sufficere motivum in dubitatione expressum, ut Missionarii* (*quantum in se est*) *ab his abstineant. Curandum ergo ut tam salubres ritus, et coeremoniae introducantur, et observentur; ac Missionarii tali circumspectione illa admininistrent, hominesque talibus instruant documentis, ut ab omni suspicione inhonestatis liberentur.*"[52] This decree of the Sacred Congregation lays down, therefore, the attitude which individual ministers must take regarding the use of the Sacramentals constituted by the Church. They cannot change them, omit them or abolish them at will. A constitution of Pope Paul III of 1537, upon which the above decree is in part based,

---

49. Ex Bulla Pii IV, "*Iniunctum nobis,*" 13 Nov. 1564, Denz. Bann. 994.
50. Bellarmine, *op. cit.*, lib. II, pp. 140-145.
51. Augustine, *op. cit.*, vol. IV, p. 559.
52. S. C. de Prop. Fide (Sinarum), 12 sept., 1645, ad 2.—Coll. 114.

the anointing or the breathing be regarded as inapt and unfit for the sacramental ceremonies of Baptism and as altogether improper for Baptism. The missionaries were charged at the same time to instruct the people of these districts and use every effort to remove the aversion of the people for the rites and then to notify the Holy See within ten years concerning the state of affairs.[56]

This decree was reinforced by a later Apostolic letter of the same Pontiff, entitled "*Concredita nobis*" of May 13, 1739, where the Pope appeals to the enforcement of his previous injunctions. ". . . *Demandamus et praecipimus, ut omnia et singula quae in dictis nostris Litteris continentur, integre, exacte, ac inviolabiliter observetis, atque ab eis quorum cura ad vos spectat, remota penitus quavis aliter interpretandi potestate, adamussim observari faciatis, in virtute sanctae obedientiae, sub poena suspensionis ab exercitio pontificalium interdicti ab ingressu Ecclesiae et respective excommunicationis latae sententiae* . . . ."[57]

Five years later, on Sept. 12, 1744, appeared the constitution, "*Omnium Sollicitudinum,*" of Benedict XIV, wherein the learned Pope calls attention to the dispensations given by Pope Clement XII regarding the omission of the above mentioned Sacramentals in the administration of Baptism. Urging the missionaries to exert every possible effort in bringing about a proper attitude among the pagan tribes in question, he, for the same reasons that moved Clement to absolve from the administration of these Sacramental rites, prorogues the faculty for the missionaries for another ten years. Allowing that a threatening danger to the best interests of the Christian religion would be occasioned by the rigid insistence upon all the Sacramental rites, the Pontiff

56. Clemens XII, *litt. ap.* "*Compertum,*" 24 aug., 1734. *Fontes,* n. 296.
57. Clemens XII, *litt. ap.* "*Concredita Nobis,*" 13 maii, 1739. *Fontes,* n. 300.

hopes that gradually those tribes will be attuned to the Christian spirit so that the Sacraments may be correctly and becomingly administered. The missionaries are therefore again reminded by him, not to use these faculties: *"Nonnisi certis in casibus, et cum gravis id necessitas postulabit, de quo eorum conscientiam oneramus."*[58]

These documents offer therefore a convincing proof of the claim made by canon 1146, that the Church can abolish the Sacramentals, can change them, as well as their manner of administration. It must also be clear that this power belongs to the Holy See exclusively, and that such changes are made only after due deliberation, and under pressing circumstances.

2. Difference, *ratione effectus*

Besides the distinction thus far pointed out, a second difference arises between the Sacraments and the Sacramentals, by reason, namely, of the effect produced. It is an article of Catholic Faith, that the Sacraments, when worthily received, infallibly confer the Sacramental and the sanctifying Grace: *"Si quis dixerit, non dari gratiam per huiusmodi Sacramenta semper et omnibus, quantum est ex parte Dei, etiamsi rite ea suscipiant, sed aliquando et aliquibus A. S."*[59] Baptism, Confirmation and Holy Orders confer, besides the Grace, also a character upon the soul, according to the same Council.[60] These graces and the character are conferred by the Sacraments directly and immediately. Sin is removed by them. The Sacramentals, on the other hand, do not infuse Sanctifying Grace, or impress a character upon the soul. They

58. Benedictus XIV, Const. *"Omnium Sollicitudinum,"* 12 sept., 1744, n. 31 & 32. *Fontes,* n. 348.

59. Conc. Trent, sess. VII, *de sacramentis in genere,* c. 7. Denz.-Bann. n. 850.

60. Conc. Trent, sess. VII, *de sacramentis in genere,* c. 9. Denz.-Bann. n. 852.

do not remit sin immediately.[61] Still, the Sacramentals may and do confer some actual graces, especially such as are necessary for leading a good Christian life.[62] For which reason the Church has instituted special Sacramentals for those that enter upon a new state in life, *viz.*, Nuptial Blessing, Tonsure, etc. The Sacramentals also immunize the recipient to a certain extent from the influences of the evil spirit.[63] Concerning this more will be said later, under the heading of "Exorcism." Furthermore, the Sacramentals obtain God's blessings upon temporal affairs (*Largitio boni temporalis*). "*Operatio boni temporalis ut sanitatis aliorumve beneficiorum.*"[64] "*Die Sakramentalien haben die Kraft, natuerliche und uebernatuerliche, leibliche und geistige Uebel von dem Menschen abzuwenden.*"[65] The Sacramentals serve, therefore, to take away from the pious user, the "*mala praesentia*," whether they are of body or soul, temporal or spiritual, and to preserve him from like future evils.[66] And lastly, the Sacramentals take away venial sins.[67] Practically all approved authors are agreed on this. Yet the exact manner in which this last result is realized is not easily established, and has elicited some discussions on the part of theologians.[68] St. Thomas offers an acceptable reason when he discusses about the remission of venial sin. He enumerates three ways in which venial sins are remitted and states: ". . . . *Benedictio episcopalis, aspersio aquae benedictae, quaelibet sacramentalis*

61. Pohle-Preuss, *Sacraments*, vol. I, pp. 117-119.
62. Cappello, *De Sacr.* vol. I, n. 106. Genicot, *Institutiones Theo. Mor.*, vol. II, n. 107. St. Thomas, III, q. 65, a. 1.
63. St. Thomas, 2-2, q. 90, a. 2; Cappello, *De Sacr.*, vol. I, n. 107. Laymann, *Theo. Mor.*, lib. V, tit. IX, cap. 13.
64. Noldin, *op. cit.*, vol. III, no. 48.
65. Schmid, *Sakramentalien d. Kath. Kirche*, p. 42.
66. Pohle-Preuss, *op. cit.*, vol. I, pp. 117-119. Noldin, l. c. Cappello, *op. cit.*, vol. I, n. 108. *Arendt De Sacramentalibus*, n. 225.
67. Acta et Decr. Conc. Pl. Balt. II, cap. X, p. 178. Bellarmine, *op. cit.*, Tom. III, lib. II, cap. 31.
68. St. Alphonsus, lib. IV, tract. I, c. 4.

unctio, oratio in Ecclesiae dedicata et si aliqua alia sunt eiusmodi operantur ad remissionem peccatorum venialium."[69] The manner in which this takes place is given by Cappello and many others, though, as stated above, all are not agreed. "*Non enim causant gratiam, sed excitant rationem ad aliquid considerandum quod excitat charitatis fervore, et etiam pie creditur quod virtus divina interius operetur excitando dilectionis fervorem . . . et hoc modo aqua benedicta, benedictio pontificalis et huiusmodi Sacramentalia causant remissionem venialis peccati.*"[70] Dr. Schmid is very clear in his opinion: "*Durch die Anwendung der Sakramentalien werden die der Suende enteggenstehenden Akte erweckt; man erweckt einen lebendigen Glauben, setzt sein Vertrauen auf den Herrn und wended sich zu Ihm in heiliger Liebe, und verdraengt dadurch die laeszlichen Suenden, da jene Akte nich sein koennen ohne wahre Reue ueber jede Beleidigung Gottes.*"[71] Hence the Sacramentals remit venial sins, not exactly *per se*, or immediately, but only in as far as they dispose the recipient to the acts necessary for the remission of sins. "*Wer sie ohne Zerknirschung, ohne Glauben empfangen wuerde, bei dem duerfte diese Wirkung so wenig eintreten, wie bei dem, der sie night in Stande der Gnade empfaengt.*"[72]

The remission of venial sins, effected by the Sacramentals, would, however, not imply the cancellation of temporal punishment due to sin.[73] The more common opinion seems to deny that the temporal punishment is in any direct way affected by the Sacramentals. The opinion finds support in the fact that the Sacramentals were not instituted for this purpose or end. Still, it goes

69. St. Thomas, III, q. 87, 3.
70. St. Thomas, *De Malo*, q. 7, a. 12. Cappello, *op. cit.*, vol. I, n. 105. Noldin, *op. cit.*, vol. III, n. 48. Ferraris, *sub verbo "Peccatum."*
71. Schmid, *op. cit.*, p. 50.
72. Schmid, l. c. Pohle-Preuss, *Sacraments*, vol. I, p. 119.
73. Cocaleo, *Tent. Theo. Moral. Tom. III*, Disc. III, c. 3.

without saying that the Church might attach an indulgence to a Sacramental, and thus effect the remission of the temporal punishment.[74] "*Sic igitur certum est, potuisse Pontificem applicare huiusmodi satisfactionis partem homini utenti hoc vel illo Sacramentali . . . . quae applicatio si fiat, erit per modum indulgentiae; nec video quomodo possit aliter per Ecclesiam attribui his Sacramentalibus. An vero hoc modo sint aliqua sacramentalia instituta ad hunc finem, et ad hunc effectum illo modo tribuendum mihi non satis constat; nec video quo fundamento sufficienti affirmari possit.*"[75] St. Thomas, too, denies that the Sacramentals, *per se* or directly, remit the temporal punishment. "*. . . . Non autem per quodlibet praedictorum semper tollitur totus reatus poenae . . . sed reatus poenae remittitur per praedicta secundum motum fervoris in Deum . . . .*"[76] Schmid seems to hold that the temporal punishment is removed in a manner similar to venial sins: "*Auf aehnlicher Weise verhaelt es sich mit Nachlassung der zeitlichen Strafen, indem der Empfang der Sakramentalien mit innern und aeuszeren Buszakten verbunden ist; innerlich, Reue, Zerknirschung, Schmerz, aeuszerlich, Gehorsam unter die Kirche, Demuetigung seines Verstandes, Verlaeugnung des Eigenwillens, wodurch Gottes Gerechtigkeit gesuehnt wird.*"[77]

The effects of the Sacramentals as a whole would, therefore, depend upon the intention of the Church, that is to say, the intention which the Church had in instituting or receiving them. The Sacraments depend in their effect entirely upon the will of Christ. Some of the Sacraments were instituted to confer the First Grace, others to confer the Second Grace. They are dependent

---

74. Pesch. *Prael. Dog.*, vol. VI, n. 343.
75. Suarez, *op. cit.*, vol. XX, Quest. LXV, Disp. XV, sect. 3, n. 9.
76. St. Thomas, III, q. 87, a. 3 ad 3.
77. Schmid, *op. cit.*, c. III. Pruemmer, *Manuale Theo. Mr.* Tom. III, app. De Sacramentalibus.

in their effect entirely upon the intention of their institutor. Similarly, the Sacramentals depend in their effect, upon the intention of the Church.[78] It follows, therefore, that the single Sacramentals will not produce all these effects, but each will produce the peculiar effect intended by the Church when instituting the Sacramentals.[79]

3. Difference, *ratione modi operandi*

Sacraments produce their effect "*ex opere operato.*" When validly received (by "*non ponentibus obicem*") they infallibly produce their effects by reason of the work of Redemption of our Divine Saviour. "*Si quis dixerit, Sacramenta novae legis non continere gratiam, quam significant, aut gratiam ipsam non ponentibus obicem non conferre . . . . A. S.*" "*Si quis dixerit, per ipsa novae legis sacramenta ex opere operato non conferri gratiam sed solam fidem divinae promissionis ad gratiam consequendam sufficere A. S.*"[80] Sacramentals produce their effect not "*ex opere operato,*"[81] but "*ex opere operantis* (*ecclesiae*)."[82] They operate by reason of the supporting prayer of the Church. When the Church makes use of Sacramentals she either "*formaliter*" or "*virtualiter*" asks God to grant a certain effect, and it is in virtue of this prayer of the Church, that the Sacramentals operate.[83] If the effect of the Sacramentals depended principally upon the "*opus operans*" of the subject, then any good work might properly be called

---

78. Suarez, *op. cit.*, vol. XX, Quest. LXV, Disp. XV, sect. 3, n. 8.
79. Suarez, *op. cit.*, vol. XX, Quest. LXV, Disp. XV, sect. 3, n. 1. Noldin, *op. cit.*, vol. III, n. 48.
80. Conc. Trident. sess. VII, *de sacramentis in genere*, c. 6 & 8.
81. Bellarmine, *op. cit.*, lib. II, cap. 31.
82. Acta et Decreta Conc. Pl. Balt. II, n. 341. Pohle-Preuss, l. c. Noldin, *op. cit.*, vol. III, n. 44. Some Theologians hold indeed that the Sacramentals too produce their effect "*ex opere operato,*" but they are in the minority.
83. Vermeersch-Creusen, *Epitome J. Canonici*, vol. II, n. 463. Pesch, Prael. Dog. vol. VI, n. 338.

a Sacramental, there would be no reason for the distinction between a good work, a pious act and a Sacramental.[84] This is evidently the spirit of the canon: "*Quibus ecclesia uti solet ad obtinendos ex sua impetratione effectos praesertim spirituales.*" Bellarmine maintained staunchly that the Church had the power of instituting Sacramentals that would and could work "*ex opere operato.*"[85] But it seems that he ignored the fact that God alone can render a sensible sign efficacious of grace, no matter whether this grace be sanctifying or second grace. The Sacramentals, being instituted by the Church, cannot have this effect "*vi institutionis.*" Coninck, in treating of the Sacraments, gives an interesting view when he maintains that just as the Church cannot institute signs that confer sanctifying grace (since God alone can confer sanctifying grace), so is it beyond the Church's power to institute any signs that confer or might confer other graces.[86]

Granting now that the Sacramentals operate "*ex opere operantis ecclesiae,*" it would still be unreasonable to assume that the disposition of the subject plays no part in the accomplishment of the effect.[87] In order to realize the effect of the Sacramentals the subject must be proper disposed, and remove every "*obex.*" The more favorable the disposition of the subject, the greater will the effect of the Sacramental be. This disposition must be looked upon, however, as a mere condition, and not as a matter that touches the intrinsic efficacy or virtue of the Sacramental. As far as the intrinsic and principal efficacy of the Sacramental is concerned, the spiritual condition of the minister will not enter into question. A blessing or consecration performed by an

84. Pesch, l. c.
85. Bellarmine, *op. cit.* lib. II, c. 31.
86. Pesch. *Prael. Dog.* vol. VI, n. 337. Genicot, *Instit. Theo. Mor.* vol. II, n. 107.
87. Pohle-Preuss, l. c.

unworthy minister will be efficacious as well as that of a worthy minister, for the reason that the minister acts in the name of the Church. It is the Church that blesses or consecrates.[88] "*Sacramentalia vim et efficaciam suam non habent ex sanctitate et devotione ministri.*"[89] Nevertheless, the opinion that the spiritual state of the minister has some bearing upon the efficacy of the Sacramentals is also deserving of consideration, especially as far as the expulsion of evil spirits is concerned. "*Attamen effectus sacramentalium magna ex parte pendent a dispositionibus tum ministri tum subiecti eadem suscipientis aut in usu adhibentis.*"[90]

It was stated above that the Sacraments work infallibly when worthily received. Do the Sacramentals operate similarly, that is, infallibly? Theologians are not agreed in their opinion,[91] but their difficulties are not of a very serious nature, as Vermeersch aptly remarks: "*Magis tamen verbis quam re dissentiunt.*"[92] There is place for distinction. Those Sacramentals that consist in constitutive consecrations or blessings[93] produce their effect infallibly, provided no obex stands in the way. They permanently and infallibly dedicate a person or thing to Almighty God and to the Divine Cult.[94] "*Consecratas et Benedictas esse res vel personas quas Ecclesia benedicit vel consecrat, non ambigitur, ita ut res permanenter benedictae constitutiva benedictione re vera possideant inchoativam istam virtutem supernaturalem.*[95] Sacramentals that consist in invocative blessings or consecrations are not absolutely infallible in their effects.[96] These latter kind of Sacramentals,

88. Pruemmer, *Man. Theo. Mor.*, vol. III, append. de Sacramentalibus.
89. Noldin, *op. cit.*, vol. III, n. 50.
90. Cappello, *De Sacramentis*, vol. I, n. 102.
91. Laymann, *Theo. Moral.* lib. V, tit. IX, cap. 13. St. Alphonsus, lib. VI, tract. I, cap. 4.
92. Vermeersch-Creusen, *Epitome*, J. Can. vol. II, n. 463.
93. Wernz, *Jus. Decr.* Tom. III, n. 758. Canon. 1488.
94. Genicot, *Instit. Theo. Moral.*, vol. II, n. 107.
95. Vermeersch-Creusen, *Epitome, J. Can.* vol. II, n. 463.
96. Genicot, l. c.

by their very nature, are destined to obtain, through the bounty of God, spiritual or temporal favors upon persons or things. Now, although it is commonly held, that the prayers of the Church, as the Spouse of Christ (by reason of which the Sacramentals operate), are never in vain and always most acceptable to Almighty God,[97] it cannot be maintained that for this reason they will always produce the *determined* effect, that the minister or the recipient of the Sacramental may *directly* intend.[98] In teaching that the Sacramentals operate infallibly, authors do not restrict this infallibility as regards invocative blessings and consecrations to a *definite* or *particular* effect. For it stands to reason that God cannot grant a favor by reason of a Sacramental that would be contrary to His Wisdom and Providence, and harmful to the recipient of the Sacramental. *"Cum enim omnia Sacramentalia ultimo tendere debeant ad gratiam sanctificantem procurandam aut augendam si huic fine obsit, vel dispositio hominis vel bonum temporale petitum per Sacramentalia, tunc non producitur effectus."*[99] Dr. Schmid adds an interesting remark: *"Stellt man nun noch die Frage, warum die Sakramentalien so selten oder gar nicht die gennanten Wirkungen hervorbringen, so kann sie, wenn sie als Einwurf gelten sollte die erste Bestimmung derselben auch die Natur zu heiligen und tauchliche Elemente fuer gottesdienstliche Handlung zu schaffen, nicht beruehren, denn diese wird immer erreicht; was die Kirche segnet ist gesegnet. Die Frage kann nur ihre sekundaere Bestimmung im Augen haben, jene Wirkungen naemlich, die am Menschen hervorgebracht werden und an seinen Guetern.*[100]

97. Bellarmine, *op. cit.*, lib. II, cap. 31.
98. St. Alphonsus, lib. VI, tract. I, cap. 4.
99. Pruemmer, *Man. Theo. Moral.* vol. III, n. 92. Vermeersch-Creusen, *Epitome, J. Can.* vol. II, n. 463. Arendt, *De Sacramentalibus*, p. 273.
100. Schmid, *op. cit.*, p. 54.

CHAPTER IV

The Minister of the Sacramentals in General

Canon 1146: *"Legitimus Sacramentalium minister est clericus, cui ad id potestas collata sit quique a competente auctoritate ecclesiastica non sit prohibitus eandem exercere."*

The administration of the Sacramentals is a ministerial act, exercised in the name of the Church, and hence requires the powers of Orders.[1] But since clerics alone can obtain this power of Orders,[2] it follows that clerics alone can be the legitimate ministers of the Sacramentals. The term cleric stands here, in this canon in opposition to laic, and comprises all those who have been bound to the Divine Ministry by the reception of first Tonsure.[3] It must be taken in the strict sense, and not in the sense of the Old Law, when even those who devoted themselves to a religious life or consecrated themselves in some manner or other to a spiritual cause, were politely called clerics.[4] Laics are therefore definitely excluded from the administration of the Sacramentals. This matter has been very plainly settled by a decree quoted in the Decretals of Gregory IX. The case concerned certain Abbesses, in the diocese of Burgos and Palencia, who were in the habit of blessing their nuns, of hearing their confession in criminal cases, and preaching and reading

1. Laymann, *Theo. Moral.* lib. V, Tit. IX, cap. 13. Cappello, *De Sacramentis,* vol. I, n. 114. *"Ideo ipse (clericus) solus, et non laicus."* —Noldin, *Summa Theo. Moral.,* vol. III, n. 46. *"Laici ergo sacramentalia conficere nequeunt."*—Vermeersch-Creusen, *Epitome,* II, n. 465.
2. Canon 118.
3. Canon 108.
4. Moroto, *Institutiones Juris Canonici,* Tom. I, p. 565.

the Gospel in public services. On being informed of this fact the Pope ordered the practice to be quashed: *"Quum igitur id absonum sit pariter et absurdum (nec a nobis aliquatenus sustinendum), discretioni vestrae per apostolica scripta mandamus, quatenus, ne id de cetero fiat, auctoritate curetis apostolica firmiter inhibere, quia licet beatissima Virgo Maria dignior et excellentior fuerit Apostolis universis, non tamen illi sed istis Dominus claves regni coelorum commisit."*[5]

The same point is borne out by a decree of the Sacred Congregation of Rites of July 5, 1892. The question was raised by certain missionaries laboring in the central portion of Tonkin, concerning the conducting of exequies by a catechist. The missionaries pointed out the difficulties of travel, especially during times of persecutions, and called attention to the fact that frequently the faithful would have to be buried without the last rites, *i. e.,* without any exequial services, unless the catechists would be allowed to perform these services, and that Catholics were accused by the infidels of not showing due respect to their dead. The missionaries stated that a custom existed, but that it was not certain as to whether an apostolic indult had been granted, although the impression was current that such an indult had been obtained.

The response of the Congregation ordered that the custom should by all means be abolished. It granted, however, with the view of avoiding all difficulties, that in the proposed cases the catechists might kneel down and recite either alone or alternately with the bystanders, the *"De Profundis,"* together with the respective

5. C. 10, X, *de poenitentiis et remissionibus,* V, 38.

orations, over the corpse and grave, and then, without the use of any prayer, sprinkle Holy Water over them.[6]

The power of Orders required in the cleric will depend upon the nature of the Sacramental to be administered, as shall be shown in subsequent chapters. "*Noverit sacerdos quarum rerum Benedictiones ad ipsum et quae ad Episcopum suo jure pertineant, ne majoris dignitatis munera temere, aut imperite unquam usurpet propria auctoritate.*"[7] In the Decretals attention is called to the propriety of consecrating temples, vessels, altars, etc., to the exclusive service of God. The canon points out that the practice of such consecration existed under the Old Testament, by special Divine Command, and that special rites were exercised, by divinely appointed ministers for these consecrations. It insists that since the New Testament is the realization of the promises made under the Old Testament, these consecrations are all the more in place, and that they should be performed by special ministers, namely, by Bishops: "*Cratis ab Episcopis et non a chorepiscopis* (*quo saepe prohibiti sunt, nisi ut predictum est summa necessitate exigente.*"[8] In as far as the minister acts in the name of the Church, his power regarding the Sacramentals will depend upon the commission which he has received from the Church. "*Absque commissione ecclesiae Christi, ea* (*sacramentalia*) *conferre non valet.*"[9] The reason of this is to be found in the fact that the effect of the Sacramentals depends upon the intercession of the Church. Hence it is that the Church can and does strictly

6. S. R. C. Tunkini Centralis, 5 jul. 1892. "*Resp. Consuetudinem, uti iacet, esse omnino eliminandam. Nihilominus, ut inconvenientibus, de quibus in dubio, eatur obviam, Sacra Rituum Cong. censuit proponi posse catechistis in casu exposito, ut genuflexi, vel soli feretrum aut super sepulcum psalmum 'de Profundis' cum respectiva oratione, et deinde sub silentio aquam lustralem super illa effundant.*" Coll. n. 1801.
7. Rituale Rom., Tit. VIII, c. I, *de benedictionibus regulae generales*, n. 1.
8. C. 2, D. I, *de cons.* (Exodus, XL, 9.)
9. Arendt, *De Sacramentalibus*, p. 389.

and properly forbid some clerics to administer the Sacramentals. Canon 2261 regulates that an excommunicated cleric shall not administer the Sacramentals, unless the faithful, for a good reason, ask him. This is a prohibition affecting the licitness of the administration, rather than the validity of the Sacramental,[10] since the power of Orders is not lost.[11] Yet for that reason we would not be allowed to regard the canon of small import.[12] The law grants the faithful the privilege, even in the face of this prohibition, to ask for the Sacramentals from the hands of a minister who has been forbidden the administration, whenever a just cause is present. By this just cause must be understood any good reason, concerning which the faithful themselves may judge. "Any reason (cause) may be called just, which promotes devotion or wards off temptations or is prompted by real inconvenience; for instance, if one does not like to call another minister."[13] "Or also the intention to receive frequently, etc. . . ."[14] This legislation is effective especially, then, when no other priest in good standing can be had. Should the priest in question be "*excommunicatus vitandus*" or be excommunicated by a condemnatory or declaratory sentence of an ecclesiastical court, the faithful would not be allowed to ask him for the Sacramentals except in case of danger of death, and then only when no other non-excommunicated minister is present. The regulation does not demand that a priest in good standing must be called, but merely deals with the case where no such minister is at hand.[15] All those laboring under a personal interdict, as well

---

10. Vermeersch-Creusen, *Epitome J. Can.* vol. III, n. 463.
11. Augustine, *Comm. on Canon Law*, vol. VIII, p. 182.
12. Cappello, *De Censuris*, n. 36 & 37.
13. Augustine, *op. cit.*, vol. VIII, p. 182.
14. Vermeersch-Creusen, *op. cit.*, vol. III, n. 463.
15. Augustine, *op. cit.*, vol. VIII, p. 183.

as those who are completely suspended from office, fall under this prohibition.[16]

This leads to the conclusion that a cleric may be forbidden the administration of the Sacramentals either directly or indirectly by the Church, which prohibition may arise from the law itself, be it general or particular, or from a special injunction given by competent ecclesiastical superiors. An instance of this may be found in the Decretals. The canon in question states that if any bishop who has been condemned by a synod, shall attempt to exercise any sacred function, no hope of restitution or chance of satisfaction shall be given him in a subsequent synod. *"Si quis episcopus damnatur, a sinodo, vel si presbiter aut diaconus a suo episcopo et ausi fuerint aliquid de ministerio sacro cintingere, sive episcopus juxta precedentem consuetudinem, sive presbiter aut diaconus, nullo modo liceat ei, nec in alia sinodo, spem restitutionis aut locum satisfactionis habere, sed et communicantes ei omnes abici de ecclesia oportet, ex maxime si postquam didicerint adversus memoratos prolatam fuisse sententiam eisdem communicare temptaverint."*[17]

16. Canon 2260, §2; 2275 §2; 2279 cf. Augustine, *op. cit.*, vol. VIII, on these canons.

17. C. 6, V. XI, q. 3.

PART II

CHAPTER I

Benedictions

Historical Note:

Our word *benediction*—Latin *benedictio*—is and has in the past been used by both profane and sacred writers for a large and diversified class of concepts. Its exact meaning in each case can be rightly determined only by a close study of the nature of the subject matter under discussion, general context and the like. Etymologically speaking, it is, of course, derived from the Latin *bene* and *dicere*, and in general was used by the writers of the earlier centuries to replace the Greek term, "*Eulogia*." Among the Hebrews of the Old Testament, a benediction was ordinarily regarded as a certain form of prayer, whereby God was asked to confer special benefits. Also, the conferring of these benefits and favors themselves was called a benediction or blessing. "And God blessed them, saying, increase and multiply and fill the earth and subdue it, etc. . . ."[1] Again, to praise God, to honor Him, was said to "*benedicere Deo.*"[2] "*Benedicere Deo est confiteri laudes ejus, sed benedicere Deum est facere bonum.*"[3] The custom in vogue among the Jews and early Christians of greeting each other with pious salutations was also termed a "*benedictio,*" or, as Tertullian calls it, a "*Sacramentum conversationis.*"[4]

1. Gen. I, 28.
2. Cf. Chrysost. in Ps. 144, n. 1, MPG, LV, 465.
3. St. Thomas in Ps. 33, principio.
4. Tertullian ad Marc. MPL, II, 419.

Catalanus sums up the various kinds of benedictions into three groups. "*Benedicere tria potissimum significat: 1) bene loqui de aliquo, seu aliquem laudare et commendare; 2) bona et prospera alicui precari et fausta ominari; 3) consecrare et sanctificare, seu conferre aliquod esse sacrum rei, quae benedicitur, ut fiat conveniens et apta materia sacramenti, vel sacrificii, vel fiat instrumentum salutis sive animarum sive corporum.*"[5] Ferraris gives a very commendable classification when he divides the benedictions into 1) enuntiative, 2) optative, 3) imperative.[6] In Psalm 33 we may find an illustration of the enuntiative benediction: "*Benedicam Dominum in omni tempore, semper laus in ore meo.*" Whereas Psalm 127 shows an optative benediction: "*Benedicat tibi Dominus ex Sion, et videas bona Jerusalem omnibus diebus vitae tuae.*" The imperative benediction is imparted by God either directly or indirectly, that is through the ministers of His Church, to produce a certain effect: "*Est benedictio quam dat solus Deus per se vel per ministros suos, et operatur praedictos effectus, et hanc quandoque Deus dedit per seipsum, Gen.* 1, 28, *Benedixitque ille Deus et ait, etc. . . . vel Josue XXIV*, 10, *Per illum benedixi vobis et liberavi vos.*"[7]

Here, of course, benediction stands for a religious function or ceremony, or prayer and acts, whereby the grace of God is called down upon the person or things blessed. With this signification we find benedictions, not merely in the Old Testament, but we note it even in the idolatrous cult of Rome and Greece.[8] Under the Old Law special blessings were prescribed, certain formulas had to be used.[9] It was the general law that

5. Catalanus, *Rituale Romanum*, Tom. II, p. 1.
6. Ferraris, *Prompta Bib. sub verbo "Benedictio."*
7. Ferraris, *Prompta Bib.* vol. I, p. 531.
8. Augusti, *Christliche Archäologie*, III, 390.
9. Lev. IX, 22; Num. VI, 22.

only priests could conduct these benedictions,[10] and on the more solemn occasions the High priest was to impart them.[11] At these functions the hands were extended[12] unless, indeed, only one single individual was blessed, in which case the hands were imposed as is done even today.[13]

The power of blessing residing in the priesthood of the Old Testament did not die with the Old Law, but entered into the new with notable changes. "*Mutatae sunt in alias oeconomiae novae proportionatas.*"[14] As was but fitting, the New Testament, far from abolishing the rite of benedictions, rather increased the number of blessings and stressed their importance and value. As the priests of the Old Testament were empowered to bless, so should those of the new receive this power, even in a higher and more perfect degree. "For every priest taken from among men, is ordained for men, in the things that pertain to God."[15] Christ Himself, the High Priest of the New Law, frequently imparted His Benediction. In Matt. XIX, 15, He blesses the people. Again, we read that He blesses bread and fishes.[16] At the Last Supper He blesses the Eucharistic Bread and Wine. And He reserves not this power to Himself, but lovingly communicates it to His Apostles. He first of all gives them the example: "*at vero Christus ipse Apostolos suos etiam exemplo docere voluit qua ratione benedicendi potestatem in omnium beneficium exercere deberent. Unde suavissimum sui exhibuit spectaculum parvulis manus imponentis ac benedicentis.*"[17] Furthermore, He tells them before sending them, "All power is given to

10. Deut. X, 8.
11. II Paral. XXX, 27.
12. Lev. IX, 22. Luke XXIV, 20.
13. Gen. XXVII, 4. Cf. Arendt, *op. cit.*, p. 199.
14. Arendt, *op. cit.*, p. 163.
15. Heb. V, 1.
16. Matt. XIV, 19.
17. Arendt, *op. cit.*, p. 198.

me in Heaven and on Earth," indicating that the powers which He had exercised as supreme High priest, should also be exercised by them. And finally we see the direct and incontrovertible commission, in Matthew's Gospel: "And when you come into the house salute it, saying, Peace be to this house, and if that house be worthy, your peace shall come upon it, but if it be not worthy your peace shall return to you."[18] Christ speaks here, not of a mere pious greeting, of the Eulogia, but rather of a real benediction, which was to impart grace, depending upon the disposition of the subjects, that is, of the inmates of the house. "*Dicimus traditam fuisse hisce verbis a Christo potestatem ministerialiter et exigitive benedicendi.*"[19] "*Salutatio haec non est illa communis quae de more fit, sed ut sequentibus ostenditur est precatio et benedictio qua illis pax Messianica omnium bonorum quae compendium efflagitatur.*"[20]

The power thus entrusted to the Apostles was evidently exercised by them, as is seen from the manner in which the Apostles, especially St. Paul, as a rule, begins and concludes his epistles: "Grace to you and Peace from God our Father, and from the Lord Jesus Christ."[21] Peter and John make use of similar expressions. "*Huiusmodi formulae non sunt merae salutationes . . . Iamvero ex ipso contextu satis apparet eas non esse exclusive adprecationes, sed vere ministeriales benedictiones.*"[22] The Apostles naturally communicated this power to impart benedictions to those who succeeded them in the ministry. The history of the primitive ages bears ample witness to this effect. For example, the blessing of Baptismal Water and the Sacred Oils. St.

---

18. Matt. X, 13-14.
19. Arendt, *op. cit.*, p. 190.
20. Knabenbauer, p. 387, *apud Arendt*, p. 192.
21. I Cor. I, 3. Gal. VI, 18.
22. Arendt, *op. cit.*, 183-184.

Basil assures us that this dates back to Apostolic times.[23] The heretics in the second century imitated the Christian rite of Baptism and for that purpose used water mixed with oil.[24] Cyprian denies to the Gnostics the power of validly consecrating the sacred oils.[25] Theodotus tells us about the exorcism of the Baptismal water, and says that it is sanctified.[26] Finally St. Jerome chides the deacons because they took it upon themselves to administer blessings whilst priests were present, and thereby violated the prescriptions of the Constitution of the Apostles, which provided that priests should rather bless the deacons.[27] In the Constitutions of the Apostles we read the following instructions for the Pontifex: "*Precatus pacem populo benedicat ei, ut Moyses sacerdotibus praecepit ut his verbis populo benedicerent, Benedicat tibi Deus . . .*" The law for the reception of Catechumens is in support of this; the deacon directs the Catechumen, saying: "*Surgite catechumeni, pacem Dei per Christum petite . . . . inclinate et accipite benedictionem . . .*"[28]

We have, therefore, explicit mention of benedictions being used in early history of the Church. However, the benedictions of this age were not merely confined to persons, but to objects as well, as is seen from the blessings of Baptismal Water and the Holy Oils. The blessings of "First Fruits" dates back very far, so that St. Paul seems to have followed the example of Christ, when he takes bread and gives thanks to God before eating.[29] And the Apostolic Constitutions favor us with a short prayer or blessing prescribed before meals.[30]

---

23. *De Spiritu Sancto,* MPL, IV, p. 187.
24. Irenaeus, *Contra Haereses,* MPG, VII, p. 663.
25. Cyprian, Ep. 70, MPL, IV, p. 408.
26. Tertullian, *De bapt.* c. 5, MPL, I.
27. St. Jerome, Ep. 146, MPL, XXII, 1194-1195.
28. Const. Apost. 1, VIII, c. 6 & 7, MPG, I, 1075.
29. Acts, XXVII, 35.
30. Const. Apost. l. 7, c. 49. vide also c. 3 & 4, MPG, I, 1058, 1002.

It is of utmost import to bear in mind, however, that not all of these benedictions were really Sacramentals. Evidently the benedictions of the Old Testament could not belong to the class of Sacramentals.[31] The blessings of Christ, as well as those which the Apostles administered before the institution of the Church, were not, strictly speaking, Sacramentals. No doubt these blessings were very effective, but their efficacy was derived from a charisma, rather than from the supporting prayer of the Church. "*Ideo v. g. potestas expellendi daemones ante Christi mortem, tamquam charisma extraordinarium tantummodo exerceri potuit ab Apostolis et septuaginta duobus discipulis, quippe qui nullo ordine insigniti erant (quod Sacramentum in sua plenitudine in ultima Coena et post resurrectionem iis collatum est.) Postea vero ordinaria etiam Ordinis Potestate daemonibus aliqua speciali ratione imperarunt, uti infra explicabitur. Ita dicendum esse videtur de munere praedicandi, de potestate benedicendi, baptizandi, et si quod aliud huiusmodi tunc acceperunt atque exercuerunt.*"[32] Just where to draw the dividing line as regards Sacramental and non-sacramental benedictions of the early Christians would, of course, be a most difficult and uncertain undertaking, and would be of little practical consequence to the present study. Suffice it to say, that many of the early blessings were exercised in name of the Church and were subsequently approved or

---

31. "*Quo statuto, manifestum etiam fit qua ratione haec ministerialis benedicendi potestas Sacerdotibus V. L. collata differat a potestate ipsis etiam ordinaria, ministrandi quaedam sacramenta istius Testamenti propria. Discrimen nimirum fundamentale ex effectu immediato desumendum est, ciius hinc benedictio, inde sacramentum V. L. erat efficax. Hoc sane iustitiam legalem ex opere operato conferebat atque mediante fide operantis iustitiam poterat conferre internam. Benedictio vero in V. L. nec legalem conferebat iustitiam neque internam spiritualemque sanctificationem exigebat, sed auxilia spiritualia sufficientia ex Dei promissione, quibus si homo cooperarentur, ex opere operantis ad iustitiam consequendam vel augendam adduci poterat.*" Arendt, *op. cit.*, p. 154.

32. Arendt, *op. cit.*, p. 187.

introduced by the Church and had all the qualities requisite for a Sacramental. The blessings imparted a certain "*virtus*" to the person or thing blessed. Persons that were once blessed were advised to separate themselves from the vanities of the world and worldly pursuits. Blessed objects should be treated with reverence. Blessed objects were regarded as imparting a certain grace or "*virtus*" to the persons using them.[33]

With these preliminary historical notes in mind our attention must be turned to the definition of a benediction *as a Sacramental.* St. Thomas already affirms that benedictions belong in one sense, under the general concept of prayer. Proceeding from their nature he defines benedictions as: "*Oratio, necessitate disponens, ut id quod bonum alicui est per alium ipsi fiat.*"[34] The distinguishing characteristic of a benediction is that it produces its effect *vi sui,* that is, by its very nature. This characteristic is brought to the foreground by St. Jerome when he says: "*Neque idipsum est benedictio atque supplicium quae et nominibus et operibus procul distant, nec possunt ullo modo inter se sanari, quos sancta dividit repugnantia.*"[35] Inasmuch as the minister of a benediction acts as the representative of the Church and in the name of the Church his blessing carries a certain: "*Potestas exigitiva,*" and is no longer a *mere* prayer. "*Haec autem invocatio nominis, i. e., potestatis beneficiae Domini non est mere supplicatio nomine porrecta ecclesiae, cujus minister est sacerdos, sed intelligi debet invocatio exigitiva.*"[36] The definition given by Noldin, practically speaking, covers the notion already proposed: "*Benedictio,*" says he, "*est oratio movens alium ad conferendum alicui bonum.*" He, of

---

33. Const. Apost. l. 8, c. 29, MPG, I, 1126 & l. 7, c. 43, MPG, I, 1043. Origin, *Ad Rom.* IX, 14 MPG XIV, 1220.
34. St. Thos. IV, d. 15, q. 4, a. 1.
35. St. Jerome, ep. 100, MPL, XXII, 824.
36. Arendt, *op. cit.,* p. 136.

course, takes the words in a somewhat more liberal sense, not confining himself exactly to the notion of a benediction as a Sacramental. In consequence, he immediately proceeds to divide benedictions into clerical or ecclesiastical and lay benedictions. Here we deal, however, only with the sacramental benedictions, or what Noldin calls the *"benedictio ecclesiastica,"* and regards as a benediction performed in the name of the Church by an ecclesiastical person.[37]

Division:

The most remote classification of benedictions gave rise to two groups, namely: the *Liturgical* and the *Extra-liturgical*.[38] The liturgical benediction was always attached to some sort of liturgical exercise, and was of two kinds, the one being for the entire community, and the other was prescribed for the reception and dismissal of catechumens and for the administration of the Sacraments.[39] The extra-liturgical benedictions were performed outside and separate of regular liturgical functions, and were customarily divided into blessings reserved to bishops, and blessings not reserved.[40]

Another ancient division of benedictions is indicated in the Constitutions of the Apostles, when it speaks of *"benedictio magna (majora)"* and *"benedictio parva."*[41] The reason of this distinction has, however, never been satisfactorily accounted for by the authors. Some say that *"benedictiones magnae"* were those reserved to bishops, while the *"benedictiones parvae"* could be imparted by priests.[42]

37. *"Alia dicitur ecclesiastica, quae fit a persona ecclesiastica nomine ecclesiae."* Noldin, *op. cit.*, III, n. 52. Cappello, *De Sacramentis*, I, n. 113.
38. Augusti, *Christliche Archäologie*, III, 392.
39. Augusti, *Christliche Archäologie*, l. c.
40. Const. Apost. l. VIII, c. 6, MPG, I, pp. 1075-1079.
41. Const. Apost. l. III, c. 10, MPG, I, p. 787.
42. Kraus, *Real-Encyclopaedie*, I, 150.

Finally, among the primitive divisions, there is mention of a "*benedictio publica*" and "*benedictio privata*" or "*benedictiones antiquiores*" and "*benedictiones recentiores.*"

Writers at the present time are no longer concerned about these classifications, but suggest the following groups:

Ratione Ministri:

a) Some benedictions are reserved to special ministers or orders, *e. g.*, blessing of *Agnus Dei.*

b) Non-reserved benedictions, which can be given by any priest not specially prohibited.

Ratione Subjecti: into personal, real and local benedictions.

Ratione Formae: some are real, others are verbal.

Ratione Ritus: Solemn and private, depending upon the solemnity under which they are given.

Ratione effectus: Constitutive and invocative. Constitutive benedictions are those that permanently consecrate or dedicate the subject—person, thing or place—to God. Invocative benedictions call down the "*benegnitas Dei*" upon the subject.[43]

Finally benedictions may be said to be distinguished into consecrations and blessings, properly so called.[44] Ordinarily writers in the field of moral or dogmatic theology, are little troubled about the distinction here referred to. In the domain of Canon Law and Liturgy the distinction is, however, of greater practical import as the two following chapters will show. We shall treat of each—Consecration and Benediction, properly so called—in particular.

---

43. Augusti, *Christliche Archäologie*, III, 393.
44. Catalanus, *Rituale Romanum*, Tom. II, p. 2.

CHAPTER II

CONSECRATION

A. *Notion*

A consecration, in a general sense, is the solemn setting apart of a person or thing from profane uses, for the purpose of Divine Cult.[1] As indicated above, it is generally regarded as a species of constitutive blessing. The custom of consecrating arose not exactly with Christianity, but dates back to the remotest antiquities. We find it among the Jews of the old Testament. Moses consecrated the chosen people to God, with special solemnities.[2] Priests were consecrated, and also Levites.[3] Walls of the city, temples, altars, etc., were all set aside by special rites which in a certain sense may be termed consecrations. And even the pagans had their consecrations, as for example, the Egyptians, Greeks and Romans, who dedicated their animals and first fruits to the gods.[4]

In this present study we treat of consecrations as Sacramentals only, namely, insofar as they are benedictions in which holy oil is used for the purpose of anointing.[5] Ordinarily, the solemnities of a consecration surpass those of blessings, and it is the common belief that the graces conferred by a consecration likewise surpass, in number and quality, the graces imparted by a blessing proper. Wherefore, "the profanation of a

1. *Kirchenlexicon*, vol. III, p. 955.
2. *Exodus*, XXIV.
3. *Exodus*, XXIX.
4. *Catholic Encyclopedia*, vol. IV, p. 277.
5. Cf. Augustine, *Commentary on Canon Law*, IV, 561.

consecrated person or thing carries with it a new species of sin, namely, sacrilege, which the profanation of a blessed person or thing does not always do."[6]

B. *Minister*

Consecrations are by law reserved to bishops, so that those who lack the episcopal character cannot validly administer them, unless by reason of an apostolic indult, or special concession of the law.[7] The propriety of reserving these more solemn rites, is well explained by Arendt: "*Haec autem reservatio jure divino profecto nititur quo Episcopi ad regimen constituti sunt in Ecclesia. Nam in omni societate deputatio permanens ad munera rectoribus eius fieri tantum potest. In Ecclesia ergo jure ordinario competit Episcopis qui tamen in ea exercenda non ut ministri Christi agunt, atque ut dispensatores mysteriorum Dei, sicuti in transmissione potestatis, i. e., clavis Ordinis, sed uti rectores humani et principales societatis religiosae.*"[8] Nor can the right of reserving them be questioned. The Church it is who gives the minister the power to administer the Sacramentals, and consequently it is within her jurisdiction to also restrict this power.[9] According to a time-honored maxim, consecrations are reserved to consecrated persons. "*Res consecratae a solis consecratis et sanctificatis pertractari debent.*"[10] Attempted consecrations by priests were hardly considered valid, under the former law. "*Nullus acolitorum vel subdiaconorum rem consecratam a presbitero aliis porrigat (quia aliud est minister, aliud assistens), nisi tantum supportet, quod ei sacerdos imposuerit suo ore benedictum.*"[11]

---

6. *Catholic Encyclopedia*, vol. IV, p. 277. Cf. Baruffaldo, *Ad Rituale Romanum Commentarium*, II, p. 66.
7. Canon 1147, §1.
8. Arendt, *De Sacramentalibus*, p. 393.
9. Suarez, *Opera Omnia*, vol. XX, p. 289 & vol. XVI, p. 271.
10. Cf. Baruffaldo, *op. cit.*, I, p. 87.
11. C. 1, D. XXIV.

The episcopal character seems, therefore, to be necessary for the valid and licit conducting of consecrations. Wherefore authors teach that bishops elect are not capable of functioning in this respect until they have received the episcopal consecration. "*Consecrationes ordini episcopali annexa, exerceri non possunt ab episcopo electo, et confirmato, nisi etiam consecratus sit.*"[12] Titular bishops act validly indeed, but for licit procedure need the consent of the local ordinary.[13]

Ministers that can, by privilege of the law, perform Consecrations

The canons of the Code expressly confer upon individuals of certain rank the power to consecrate. To some of these individuals all consecrations are permitted, others, in turn, share the privilege only in a defined degree. Cardinals, though they lack the episcopal character, can consecrate Churches, immovable and movable altars, sacred vessels, etc., according to canon 239, §1, n. 20. They cannot, however, consecrate the Sancta Olea, unless they themselves are consecrated bishops. In order to exercise their faculties licitly outside of their own territory, they need furthermore the consent of the local ordinary, in whose diocese they desire to function.[14] Abbots and prelates *nullius* are likewise favored by the law, to the extent that they can consecrate Churches and fixed altars, as well as movable altars, in their territory, even though they are not possessors of the episcopal consecration.[15] As to vicars apostolic and prefects apostolic—as also their pro-vicars and pro-prefects—the canons rule that they can consecrate chalices, patens and portable altars within their territory and during their term of office. Their faculties do not, however, extend

12. Laymann, *Theologia Moralis*, Tom. II, p. 381.
13. Canon 1157. Cf. Augustine, IV, 560.
14. Cf. Vermeersch-Creusen, *Epitome*, II, p. 251.
15. Canon 323, §2.

to the consecration of Churches of fixed altars. Furthermore, in the administration of such consecrations as the law allow to them, they must use oil consecrated by a bishop.[16]

Ministers that can, by reason of Apostolic Indult, perform Consecrations

The Holy Father being supreme head of the Church, and having the plenitude of power, can give to any cleric the power, and the full power, to consecrate. "*Verumtamen, nihil obstat quominus Papa ex plenitudine potestatis suae dispensare possit, et talem consecrandi potestatem simplici sacerdoti committere.*"[17] This extends to all consecrations, including the consecration of Churches and fixed altars.[18] The Abbot of Kempten in Bavaria received from Benedict XIV the indult to consecrate his own Church.[19] However, the indult to perform such consecrations must always be obtained directly, and cannot be made use of by way of commutation.[20] If obtained before the Code the indult would not be revoked by the Code, but in order to cease would need special revocation, as canon 4 of the Code provides.

At the present, priests in missionary countries at times receive the faculty from Rome to consecrate altar-stones, chalices and patens. Although the Pope may delegate a simple priest to administer the sacrament of Confirmation, practically speaking, he never empowers a priest (of the Latin Rite) to perform the consecration of the Sacred Chrism.[21] In early times these regulations were, however, not so strict. Cases seem to be on record where simple priests performed consecrations that at the

---

16. Cf. Vermeersch-Creusen, *Epitome*, II, p. 276. Cf. Canons 239, §1, n. 20; 294; 323, §2.
17. Laymann, *op. cit.*, II, p. 381.
18. Cf. Benedict XIV, "*Ex tuis Precibus,*" Nov. 16, 1748, Fontes 393.
19. Augustine, *Commentary*, VI, p. 5.
20. Augustine, *Commentary*, IV, p. 562.
21. Cf. Canon 781. Cf. Benedict XIV, "*De Syn. Dioec.*, VIII, l. 4.

present time are strictly reserved by law to the episcopal character. We need mention only the case of St. Columban who, it is said, dedicated the Church of St. Aurelia, at Bregenz, and consecrated the altar of said Church.[22]

Power of Bishops to Delegate

A local ordinary, though he be not consecrated himself, can grant permission to another bishop, duly consecrated, to perform all consecrations in his diocese that are by law reserved to the episcopal character. *"Si Ordinarius territorii character episcopali careat, ipse quidem (excepto Abbate vel Praelato Nullius) consecrationem (sacrorum locorum) peragere non poterit; ad ipsum tamen, etiam pro ecclesia regulari, spectabit designatio episcopi consecratoris. Quare ipsius licentia indigebit Praelatus regularis qui sit episcopus, ut propriam ecclesiam consecret."*[23] Without permission from the local ordinary, an extra-diocesan bishop would act illicitly, though validly, in performing consecrations. Augustine would introduce an exception here, by still claiming for religious the privilege extended to them by Leo X in the Vth Lateran Council: *"Dum intra"* of Dec. 19, 1516, §12, to the effect that in case the local ordinary, after repeated requests on the part of the Regulars, should refuse to perform the consecration (of Churches and altars) the Regulars would be permitted to call another extra-diocesan bishop to impart the consecration.[24] Vermeersch, however, thinks that the unequivocal terms of the Council of Trent,[25] which forbid foreign bishops the use of Pontificals without the consent of the local ordinary, hold also in the above case. He consequently suggests that such a case be taken to

22. Walafridus Strabo, *Life of St. Gaul*, c. 6.
23. Vermeersch-Creusen, *Epitome*, II, p. 251.
24. Augustine, *Commentary*, VI, p. 4.
25. Conc. Trident. Sess. VI, de ref. C. 5; et sess. XIV, c. 2.

Rome.[26] Titular bishops likewise need the consent of the local ordinary in order to perform consecrations licitly. Finally, it is of interest to note that a bishop commissioned to consecrate in a strange diocese, must be of the same rite as the ordinary that grants the permission. A decree of the Sacred Office under date of June 16, 1831, answered the question, whether a Catholic Coptic Bishop could be called to consecrate altar stones (SS. Lapides) and churches for Latin Catholics, by saying: "*non expedire*," indicating that the consecration would be valid indeed, but that such conduct would be hardly advisable.[27] The Code repeats the doctrine clearly in canon 1155, §2: "*Ordinarius territorii, licet charactere episcopali careat, potest cuilibet eiusdem ritus Episcopo licentiam dare consecrationes peragendi in suo territorio.*" The rite must be judged according to the place to be consecrated. "*Quare, si ecclesia graeca consecranda sit in dioecesi latina, Ordinarius loci, etsi fuerit episcopus, consecrationem istam peragere non poterit, sed episcopum graecum deputare debebit, aut indultum habere S. Sedis.*"[28]

The law itself does not grant bishops the faculty of delegating priests to perform consecrations. Hence, for this delegation, the bishops need special power from the Holy See. In the United States, bishops can, at the present time, by reason of the extraordinary faculties, delegate the vicar general or another priest "*in aliqua ecclesiastica dignitate constitutum*" to perform the consecration of both fixed and portable altars, and also the consecration of chalices and patens. Said ministers must observe, however, the rite and form of the Roman Pontifical.[29]

---

26. Vermeersch-Creusen, *Epitome*, II, p. 251.
27. Cf. Vermeersch-Creusen, *Epitome*, II, p. 251; Coll. n. 822.
28. Vermeersch-Creusen, *Epitome*, II, p. 251.
29. Cf. Hilling, *Codicis J. Canonici Supplem.*, p. 49.

CHAPTER III

BLESSINGS

The word *Blessing* is here used in contradistinction to *consecrations*, to denote a benediction in which there is no anointing with sacred oil.

Minister

Paragraph two of canon 1147 states that blessings may be performed by any priest, with the exception of those blessings reserved to the Roman Pontiff, or the bishop, or to others. The power to bless is one of the functions of the priesthood, and is included in the power of Orders. "*Quilibet sacerdos potest omnes benedictiones impertire, quae non sunt reservatae . . . . Munus benedicendi per se et proprie in genere potestatis ordinis, quam dicunt ecclesiasticae institutiones est accensendum, et generatim loquendo iuxta Pontificale Romanum ad Presbyteros spectat.*"[1] "*Sacerdotem etenim oportet offerre, benedicere, praeesse . . . .*"[2]

This power is, however, not unlimited but is restricted by common law and must be exercised according to the commission of the Church.[3] A devout remark of Catalanus seems in place: "*Quare sicut in Coelis juxta varios Angelorum ordines varia sunt munera singulorum, quum Angeli inferiorum ordinum minima nuncient, Archangeli vero suprema, juxta doctrinam Sancti Gregorii Homilia* 34 *in Evangelia, et sic diversimodo dona Dei dispensunt, ita et in Ecclesia simplices*

---

1. Carbone, *Praxis Ordinandorum*, p. 198. Cf. Const. Apost. l. VIII, c. 28, MPG, I, pp. 1123-1126.
2. *Pontificale Romanum, in ordinatione presbyteri.*
3. Cf. *Rituale Romanum*, Tit. VIII.

Sacerdotes velut Angeli inferioris ordinis ad peragendas simplices Benedictiones sunt destinati, Episcopi vero tanquam Archangeli ordinis excelsioris Benedictiones sacratiores solemnioresque perficiunt."[4]

Blessings Reserved to the Holy See

Since centuries long gone by, certain blessings have been reserved to the Supreme Pontiff, the performance of which is seldom, if ever, entrusted to inferior ministers. At the present time there are chiefly four of these.

1) The Blessing of the Pallium, which takes place on the Feast of SS. Peter and Paul, after the second Vespers. This blessing dates back to perhaps the sixth or seventh century, and has practically always been regarded as a Pontifical function, since it signifies the participation of the recipient in the supreme pastoral powers of the Pope.[5]

2) The Blessing of the Golden Rose, which is given as a sign of Good Will and Esteem to Rulers Princes, Governments, Cities, Churches, etc. At one time these Roses were sent without first being blessed. However, the ceremony of blessing the Golden Rose is now conducted annually, even though the Rose is not given away every year. The sending of the Golden Rose dates back to the eighth century. But Innocent IV, 1245-54, was the first Pontiff who blessed it, before transmitting or bestowing it.[6]

3) Blessing of the *Agnus Dei*, which takes place on Dominica in Albis, originated during the fifth century and is now reserved to the Pontiff.[7]

4) Blessing of the Royal Sword.[8]

---

4. Catalanus, *Rituale Romanum*, Tom. II, p. 4.
5. Bona, *Rerum Liturgi.*, Tom. II, p. 272. Cf. Vermeersch-Creusen, I, p. 141, footnote.
6. Amberger, *Pastoral-Theologie*, vol. II, p. 739. *Catholic Encyclopedia*, vol. VI, 629.
7. Amberger, *op. cit.*, II, p. 798.
8. *Catholic Encyclopedia*, vol. II, 600.

Blessings Reserved by Law to Bishops.

Besides the consecrations referred to above, the law reserves a number of blessings to the Bishops. The following are the chief ones.

1) The Blessing of Abbots and Prelates *Nullius*, when these by reason of an apostolic mandate, or by reason of their statutes, must receive the blessing, is to be administered by a bishop of their own choice. Other abbots cannot perform this blessing.[9] Abbots Regulars must now, according to the New Code, be blessed,[10] and this blessing is to be asked of the local ordinary, that is, the ordinary of the place in which the monastery is situated. Any other bishop would act unlawfully, without the local ordinary's consent.[11] The importance of this blessing is reflected in canon 964, No. 1: "*Abbas regularis de regimine, etsi sine territorio nullius, potest conferre primam tonsuram et ordines minores, dummodo promovendus sit ipsi subditus vi professionis saltem simplicis, ipse vero sit presbyter et benedictionem abbatialem legitime acceperit . . .*"

2) Blessing of Virgins, likewise, belongs to the bishops. At the present time this function is hardly customary except in the case of "*Abbatissarum et Monialium.*" Their blessing differs, however, somewhat from the former rite.[12] Under the Old Law we find a number of decrees warmly vindicating the rights of Bishops with regard to the "*consecratio virginum.*"[13]

---

9. S. R. C., March 8, 1617.
10. Cf. Vermeersch-Creusen, *Epitome*, I, 313.
11. Canon 625. Augustine, *Commentary*, III, 352.
12. Suarez, *Opera Omnia*, XVI, p. 492.
13. *Quamvis corepiscopis et presbiteris plurima cum episcopis ministeriorum communis sit dispensatio, quedam tamen sibi prohibita nouerint, sicut est presbiterorum et diaconorum, et virginum consecratio. . . .*" c. 4, D. LXVIII.
"*Aurelius episcopus dixit. . . Crismatis confectio, et puellarum consecratio a presbiteris non fiat*" c. 1-3, C. XXVI, q. 6. Adds Gratian: "*Puellarum tamen consecrati, episcopo consulto per presbiterum fieri valet.*"
"*Presbiter inconsuto episcopo virgines non consecret, crisma vero numquam conficiat.*" c. 2, C. XXVI, q. 6, etc.

3) The Confection of the Holy Oils and Chrism has, since remotest Christian times, been regarded as an episcopal function. The present attitude of the Church can be gathered from various canons of the Code. Canons 741 and 954 prescribe that the oil to be used for Confirmation and Extreme Unction is oil blessed by the bishop; and canon 734 sets down the general rule that the oil to be used in the administration of the Sacraments must be blessed by the bishop, who is to do this on Holy Thursday in his own rite. Priests of the Greek Church have even today the faculty of blessing the oil for Extreme Unction, before they administer the Sacrament. Hence they cannot be forced to apply to a Latin bishop for these oils, unless in those places where the ancient custom of Greek priests blessing the oil is not in force. But as regards the Sacred Chrism, this must always be obtained from a bishop, even by the Greek priests.[14] Priests are forbidden, however, to ask the Sacred Oils of a Schismatic bishop.[15] In cases where a priest administers Confirmation, either by law or by reason of an apostolic indult, he must, nevertheless, always use oil blessed by one in episcopal order.[16] A pastor, even in case of extreme necessity, cannot validly

---

14. Cf. Const. Apost. l. VII, c. 42. Clement, VIII, (*ex Instructione super ritibus Italo-Graecorum,* 30 Aug. 1595)." . . . *Non sunt cogendi presbyteri Graeci olea sancta praeter chrisma ab episcopis Latinis dioecesanis accipere, cum huiusmodi olea ab eis in ipsa oleorum et sacramentorum exhibitione, ex vetere ritu, conficiantur seu benedicantur. . . . Chrisma autem, quod non nisi ab episcopo, etiam iuxta eorum ritum, benedici potest, cogantur accipere.*" Denziger-Bannwart, n. 1086.

15. "*Non audeant tamen ab Episcopis Graecis externis Schismaticis, seu Sanctae Romanae Ecclesiae communionem non habentibus, illud accipere, vel eo uti.*" Benedict XIV, const. "*Etsi Pastoralis,* 26 maii, 1742. Fontes, n. 328.

16. Canon 781.

use oil for Extreme Unction that has been blessed by himself.[17]

4) The Dedication of Churches. A distinction must here be introduced between a solemn dedication accompanied by anointing with Holy Oil, and known as Consecration, and simple dedication, commonly called the blessing of Churches.[18] The former, only bishops and those prelates mentioned above, pages 52 & 53, can conduct. But the simple dedication is also by law reserved unto the bishop, *i. e.*, the local ordinary of the place in which the Church is located, provided the Church belongs to the secular clergy, or to non-exempt religious or to lay communities. As regards the blessing of a Church that belongs to exempt religious, it is the law that the major superior has the right to perform the blessing.[19]

5) Blessing of Cemeteries. Again there are two kinds, *viz.*, the solemn and the simple. The former is according to canons 1155 and 1156, always reserved to the local ordinary of the place in which the cemetery is located, even though this cemetery belong to exempt religious. The simple blessing of cemeteries, follows

---

17. *Ad dubium: "an in casu necessitatis parochus ad validitatem sacramenti extremae unctionis uti possit oleo a se benedicto, S. Off.* 14 Sept., 1842, *respondit," negative ad formam decreti feriae V coram SS. diei* 13 Jan., 1611, *quam resolutionem Gregorius XVI eadem die approbavit.* Denz-Bann., n. 1629.

The Holy See can of course grant a simple priest the power to bless the sacred oils. Canon 945 seems to provide for this: *"Vel a presbytero qui facultatem illud benedicendi a Sede Apostolica obtinuerit."* This power could even be given for the blessing of the sacred Chrism, altho' not all theologians would admit this. (Cf. Benedict XIV, *De Synodo Dioec.* VIII, q. 4.) (Denz-Bann. n. 98, 571, 697, 1086.) Eugene IV, *"Dec. pro Armenis"* says that the materia for confirmation is *"Chrisma confectum ex oleo . . . per episcopum benedicto,"* but Noldin, quoting the Linzer Quartalschrift, affirms that in reality little doubt can remain but that Eugene IV really did confer upon the Friar Minors the power to confect the Holy Chrism. (Linz. Quartalschrift, 1904, 805 sqq.—Noldin, II, 101.)

18. Wernz, *Jus Dec.* III, n. 436.

19. Canon 1156. Cf. canon 1176.

the rule indicated above, for the simple blessing of Churches.[20]

6) Blessing of Bells. It is the wish of Holy Mother the Church that in a Consecrated Church, the bells, too, should be consecrated. This consecration is reserved to the local ordinary.[21] In blessed Churches the bells need merely be blessed. This blessing can be conducted by the same minister that is by law entitled to bless the Church in which the bells are suspended.[22]

The Consecration of altars, immovable and movable, the consecration of chalices and patens, belong to the bishop as indicated under the caption on Consecrations, and will require no further comment here.

Power of Delegation Enjoyed by the Bishop and Religious Superiors

By common law, the bishop can delegate a priest to perform only a few of the blessings that are reserved to him. "*Ergo quaedam Benedictiones ita sunt propriae Episcoporum, ut nec ab his delegari simplicibus Sacerdotibus possint nisi auctoritate Apostolica . . . .*"[23] For example, he cannot, without Apostolic Indult, delegate a priest to bless an abbot or abbess or virgins. "*Episcopus autem non habet potestatem committendi hoc munus Presbytero, quia non potest ei committere actus ordinis Pontificalis.*"[24] Similarly regarding the blessing of Holy Oils and Chrism. But as to the blessing of Churches, the bishop, as also the religious superior, have, according to canon 1156, power to delegate. The priest delegated may be either religious or secular, either pastor or simple priest.[25] Both the bishop and religious

20. Canon 1156.
21. S. R. C. April 19, 1687.
22. Canons 1155 & 1156.
23. Catalanus, *Rituale Romanum,* Tom. II, p. 5.
24. Suarez, *Opera Omnia,* XVI, p. 492.
25. S. R. C. Oct. 7, 1645 and Aug. 7, 1875.

superior can also delegate a priest to perform the simple blessing of a cemetery, but the power for solemn blessing cannot be delegated without Apostolic Indult.[26] Finally the faculty of blessing bells may be entrusted to a simple priest.[27]

Blessings Reserved to Others

Canon 462 enumerates a few functions that are reserved by law to the pastor. Among them are the blessing of houses on Holy Saturday or other days set aside by custom, according to the law of liturgical books. The blessing of the baptismal font on Holy Saturday, and also those blessings that are conducted outside of the Church with pomp and solemnity, excluding, of course, those reserved to the bishops.

The Blessing of the *Sacra Supellex* can now be done by the pastor for all the Churches and Oratories in his territory and by rectors for their Churches. Religious superiors can bless them for their Churches and Oratories, and for the Churches of the Moniales that are under their supervision.[28] Other priests need delegation either from the bishop or from the religious superior where there is question of a Church under the care of the religious. This delegation is required, however, only for lawful procedure, and has nothing to do with the validity of the blessing.[29] It seems that the pastor would not be empowered to delegate a priest to conduct the blessing of the *Sacra Supellex,* since the canon makes express mention of the bishop. However, Cappello is inclined to the opposite opinion, whereas Vermeersch replies: *Cura tamen qua ipse Codex indicat quinam alios designare possint nobis sententiam contrariam persuaded.*

---

26. Canon 1205. Canons, 1155 & 1156.
27. S. R. C. April 14, 1885 and July 16, 1594.
28. Cf. Vermeersch-Creusen, II, 335.
29. Vermeersch-Creusen, II, 335.

Sacerdotes, ex c. 1304, 5° *ab Ordinario sunt designandi.*"[30]

The nuptial blessing is reserved to the pastor or to the priest who lawfully and validly assists at the marriage. This blessing can of course be imparted any time after the marriage, but must take place during Mass.[31] The power to impart this blessing may be delegated according to the canons that rule the assistance at matrimony. Finally, inasmuch as the Code reserves funeral services to the pastor, it follows that he, too, has the right to bless the grave, etc., according to canon 1216.[32]

Among the benedictions "*aliis reserventur,*" spoken of in canon 1147, §2, mention must yet be made of those blessings reserved to special religious orders. For example, the erection of the stations, which is reserved to the Friars Minor; blessing of Rosaries to the Dominicans, or the blessing of the Brown Scapular, which belongs to the Carmelites.[33] Outside special faculties from the Holy See, ordinaries cannot authorize priests to conduct these reserved blessings.

Blessings that are reserved, no matter to whom, even if reserved to the bishop, if given by a priest not duly authorized by competent authority, are nevertheless valid (though illicit) unless, indeed, the reservation is accompanied by an invalidating clause. Such invalidating clauses may be found in canon 39.[34] "An invalidating clause would be, '*aliter non valeant*' or one expressed by a conditional apposition.[35] At times the clause '*de consensu tamen Ordinarii loci*' is attached, which consent,

30. Vermeersch-Creusen, l. cit.
31. Decree of Holy Office, Aug. 31, 1881.
32. Canon 462, n. 5.
33. Cf. Sleutjes, for the legislation regarding the Way of the Cross. Cf. Majennies P. E. Scapular devotion, origin, legislation, etc.
34. The ablative absolute does not *per se* constitute an invalidating clause. Vermeersch-Creusen, *Epitome* I, 63.
35. Augustine, *Commentary*, IV, 564.

however, does not constitute an invalidating condition, but rather is required for licit conduct."[36] This consent can be either express, tacit or reasonably presumed.[37] Hence it is of supreme importance that the faculties be well studied to determine whether the clauses are invalidating or merely render procedure illicit.[38]

Deacons in their ordination receive the power to perform a few blessings. Most prominent among these is the blessing of the Easter Candle. The reason why this is specially set aside for deacons is very probably because of the fact that the blessing is looked upon as an "*evangelium*," a joyful message of the approaching Resurrection.[39] The blessing of the five grains of incense is not included in the power and must be done by a priest. Likewise in the administration of baptism, the deacon can, according to canon 741, impart the various blessings and pronounce the exorcism, because these belong to the rite of administration of Solemn Baptism. He is to use baptismal water and blessed salt, that have been confected by one in sacerdotal orders. The prescriptions laid down for priests in the distribution of Holy Communion must be observed also by deacons, that is, they bless the faithful before but not after the distribution; when bringing communion to the sick they give the customary blessings "*cum pyxide*."[40] When licensed to conduct funeral services, they follow the rules prescribed by liturgical books and impart the blessings

---

36. "If only the words '*de consensu Ordinarii*' without the additional '*loci*' are found in the rescript, the consent of the Religious Superior is sufficient for exempt Religious, even though the clause contains the former formula '*de consensu Ordinarii loci*' provided the faculty is to be used only for the convent, not for a public oratory." Augustine, *op. cit.*, l. cit.

37. Vermeersch-Creusen, *Epitome*, II, 248.

38. Cf. Ecclesiastical Review, Dec. 1924.

39. Amberger, *Pastoral Theologie*, II, 779.

40. S. C. R. Aug. 14, 1858. Coll. n. 1166.

demanded.[41] However, in these services, they must not wear the cope.[42]

The blessing permitted to Lectors and referred to in canon 1147 n. 4, is that of bread and *Novos Fructus*. "*Lectorem siquidem oportet . . . . et benedicere panem, et omnes fructus novos.*"[43] "*Dieses Recht wurde im Ablaufe der Zeit dem Lektor gegeben, weil Alles, was Gott erschaffen hat, geheiliget wird durch das Wort Gottes (dessen Lesung dem Lektor obliegt), und Gebet.*"[44] Exorcists receive in their ordination the power to perform exorcism, but according to the law are not allowed to exercise this power.[45]

The blessings at times performed by lay persons cannot claim attention here, because "*Laici nullam benedictionem liturgicam nullumque sacramentale perficere possunt.*"[46]

---

41. S. C. R. Aug. 14, 1858. Coll. n. 1166.
42. Carbone, *Praxis Ordinandorum*, p. 123.
43. *Pontificale Romanum, de Ordinatione Lectorum.*
44. Amberger, *op. cit.*, I, 604, footnote 6.
45. Canon 1151.
46. Pruemmer, *Manuale Theo. Moralis*, III, p. 72. "*Consuevisse etiam laicos homines non modo personas, verum etiam res praesertim comestibiles benedicere . . . sed erant hae tamen Benedictiones privatae, quibus Deus virtutem dabat, non vero solemnes, et Ecclesiasticae. . .*" Catalanus, *Rituale Rom.* II, p. 4.

CHAPTER IV

Rite to be Observed

The rites used in the execution of sacred functions during the first few centuries that followed our Lord's Ascension, were naturally simple and few in number. The administration of the Sacraments and also the Sacramentals was a brief and simple process. Tertullian complains of this fact bitterly.[1] In vain do we, therefore, look to the early centuries for a detailed ritualistic prescription regarding the administration of consecracrations and blessings. Later on, the liturgical ordinances became more imperative as these grew both in number and kind, and hence the rise and growth of the many liturgies and rituals of later days.

The first and perhaps the most common of all the ceremonies in the administration of benediction was the imposition of hands. This ceremony was carried over from the Judaism of the Old Law.[2] Later on it was replaced by the *signum crucis*: *"Ad omnem progressum atque promotum, ad omnem exitum et aditum, ad vestitum et calceatum, ad lavacra, ad mensas, ad lumina, ad cubilia, ad sedilia, quaecunque nos conversatio exercet, frontem singaculo terimus."*[3] Yet it would be wrong to maintain that the early religious functions were without any other ceremony. For in the Apostolic Constitutions we already discover definite rites prescribed for the blessing of water and the Sacred Oils.[4]

---

1. Tertullian, *de bapt.* c. 2, MPL, I, 1202.
2. Augusti, *Christliche Archäologie,* III, p. 395.
3. Tertullian, *de coron,* c. 3, MPL, II, 79.
4. Probst, *Sakramente u. Sakramentalien,* pp. 78 & 85.

Canon 1148 calls special attention to the fact that in the administration and confection of the Sacramentals the minister is to accurately observe the rites approved by the Church. This refers to the prayers to be said, as also to the ceremonies to be observed and the vestments to be worn. Thus, for example, priests that can lawfully bless the sacred vestments, must use the formula given by the *Rituale Romanum* and they are not allowed to use the form of the Pontificale.[5] *Palla and Corporale* must be blessed together, or if only one of them is blessed the priest is to observe the form of the *Rituale Romanum.*[6] In the "*benedictio tumuli parvulorum,*" no special blessing is to be looked for, but *Rituale* must be followed.[7] "*Bei der Spendung* (*der Sakramentalien*) *halte er* (*der Priester*) *sich an die Form seines Rituals, und erlaube sich nicht nach Gutbefinden Gebete zu waehlen. Er muss in Namen der Kirche beten, also so beten, wie diese es ihm in den Mund legt.*"[8] "*Nihil addendo, mutando vel auferendo.*" Only such forms of blessings are to be used, therefore, as are found in approved liturgies, chiefly the *Rituale, Missale* and *Pontificale.* As a general rule, surplice and stole are prescribed, according to the nature of the function to be performed.[9] "*Rituale Romanum probat sequentes regulas generales*: '*In omni benedictione extra Missam* (*nam in Missa sunt servandae rubricae Missalis Romani*), *Sacerdos saltem superpelliceo, et stola pro ratione temporis utatur, nisi aliter in Missali notetur. Stando semper benedicat, et aperto capite. In principio cuiusque benedictionis dicat, V. Adiutorium nostrum in nomine Domini. R. Qui fecit coelum et terram. V. Dominus vobiscum. R. Et cum spiritu tuo. Deinde dicatur oratio*

5. S. R. C., March 16, 1876. Coll. de Prop. Fide n. 1452.
6. S. R. C., Sept. 4, 1880. Dec. Auth. 3524.
7. S. R. C., Sept. 4, 1880. Coll. de Prop. Fide n. 1540.
8. Schmid, *Die Sakramentalien der Kath. Kirche,* p. 113.
9. *Rituale Romanum,* Tit. VIII, c. 1.

propria, una vel plures, prout suo loco notatum fuerit. Postea rem adspergat aqua benedicta, et ubi notatum fuerit, pariter incenset, nihil dicendo."[10] In his "*Inter Omnigenas,*" Benedict XIV appeals to the Archbishops and Bishops of Servia and neighboring countries not under any pretext to allow the introduction of new rites, ceremonies and prayers in the saying of Mass, or the administration of Sacraments, as also in the imparting of blessings and exorcisms save those found in the *Missale, Rituale* or *Caeremoniale Romanum.*[11] Similarly in the letter "*Sollicitudini.*"[12] Furthermore, a decree or instruction from the Congregation of Rites, ordered the Friars Minor of the Province of St. Leopoldi, that in the administration of general absolution to Tertiaries, a violet stole was to be used.[13] "*Es ist daher in einigen Diocesen unter Suspension geboten, sich an die Formulare des Diozesan-Rituale zu halten. So sagt unter andern das von Freysing S.* 280: *'Um jeden Miszbrauch zu entfernen und hinreichenden Vorrat von Benediktions=Formularen zu bieten, sind diese etwas mehr ausgedehnt und reichlicher fuer vershiedene Beduerfnisse eingerichtet worden, so dass wir hiermit ausdruecklich erklaeren, es seien von nun an alle andern Benediktionale, in soweit sie von dem unsrigen abweichen, und andere Benediktionen, die mit den unsrigen nicht uebereinstimmen, verboten.*"[14]

Paragraph two of this same canon 1148 emphasizes the necessity of using the proper form in the administration of consecrations and blessings, by adding the sanction, that if a form not approved by the Church be employed, the benediction is invalid, *i. e.*, "*nullius*

10. Blat, *Commentarium Text.* C. J. Canonici, lib. III, pars. I, 723.
11. Benedict XIV, *ep. encycl.* "*Inter omnigenas,*" 2 febr. 1744, §18, Fontes n. 339.
12. Benedict XIV, *ep.* "*Sollicitudini,*" 1 Oct. 1745. §43. Fontes n. 362.
13. S. R. C. Dec. 22, 1905.
14. Schmid, *op cit.*, p. 113.

effectus 'ex Ecclesiae impetratione' utpote ipsius repraesentatione non effusae."[15] Ordinances of a similar nature may readily be gleaned from the many particular legislations on this matter. Says, for example, the Diocesan Ritual of Constance: "*Wir erklaeren hiemit ausdruecklich dass fuer kuenftig alle Benediktionen, in so fern sie von den unsrigen vershieden sind, fuer die Diocese Konstanz abgeschafft, und die Benediktionen und Exorcismen, oder die vershiedenen Segnungs=und Beschwoerungsformeln, die nicht insbesondere von uns durchgesehen und gut geheiszen sind, ganzlich und bei Starafe der Suspension untersagt seien.*"[16] For the blessing of an object for which no special formula is found in any of the prescribed and approved liturgical works, the "*Benedictio ad Omnia*" is to be used. It follows that formulas of private invention, no matter how well sounding, are invalid, and that the prescription of former writers, advocation under such circumstances that the minister recite the *Asperges,* the *Miserere* and then sprinkle the object with holy water, can hardly be sponsored.[17] The reason of this paragraph can be gathered from the very nature of the formulas laid down. The form prescribed for the blessing of Holy Water would, for example, ill suit for the blessing of a different object. Nor need we wonder that formulas of private coinage stand condemned, for after all blessings and consecrations are acts of exterior worship, and must at all times bespeak orthodoxy. The great desire of unity and harmony ever manifested in the life of the Church necessarily elicits the demands of this canon.[18]

---

15. "*i. e. nullus effectus, ex Ecclesiae impetratione, utpote ipsius repraesentatione non effusae.*" Blat, *op. cit.*, p. 723.
16. Schmid, *op. cit.*, p. 113.
17. Canon 1264, §1.
18. Cf. St. Thomas, 2-2, q. 93, a. 1.

CHAPTER V

Subject and Object of Blessings

The Sacramentals, as institutions of the Church, are naturally intended principally for the spiritual and temporal needs of the faithful. "*In favorem praecipue saltem membrorum Ecclesiae.*"[1] "To you first God, raising up his Son, hath sent him to bless you; that every one may convert himself from his wickedness."[2] Hence, the canon of the Code: "*Benedictiones, imprimis impertiendae catholicis, dari quoque possunt catechumenis, imo, nisi obstet Ecclesiae prohibitio, etiam acatholicis ad obtinendum fidei lumen vel, una cum illo, corporis sanitatem.*"[3]

For their advantageous reception the proper dispositions should at all times maintain in the recipient. Authors recommend various dispositions, chief among which is a strong and unqualified faith in the Sacramentals. "*Der Empfaenger muss persoenlich glauben und vollkommner als jener* (*der Spender*), *er muss glauben, ehe er die Sakramentalien empfaengt, bei und nach dem Empfange, und muss glauben felsenfest und unershcuetterlich; unwandelbar, unfehlbar muss er die Wirkung erwarten, nicht im Gringsten schwanken oder zweifeln, oder bedenklich sein, etc. . . .*"[4] Furthermore, he must receive the blessing with humble resignation to the will of God. He must desire the effects of the Sacramentals only in as far as they will redound, at least ultimately, to his spiritual good. The well-being

1. Arendt, *De Sacramentalibus*, p. 396.
2. Acts III, 26.
3. Canon 1149.
4. Schmid, *Die Sakramentalien*, p. 86.

of the body must be sought not at the expense of the soul, but rather in as far as it will promote the well-being of the soul. Temporal blessings should be desired because of the relation that they may and should bear to the spiritual makeup of man; or if sought in themselves, they must not be asked in prejudice to the spiritual good.[5] These dispositions can, however, best maintain only in a soul free from sin, in the state of sanctifying grace. Nevertheless, sanctifying grace is no absolute requisite for the worthy and proper reception of the Sacramentals, since, as a matter of fact, the Sacramentals are administered at times for the express purpose of preparing the recipient for a worthy confession, or at least for an act of perfect contrition.[6]

Now, although, as the canon states, the faithful are, properly speaking, the subjects of blessings, since they alone can properly share in the privileges and benefits of the Church, catechumens, and even non-Catholics—unless, indeed, special prohibitions exist to the contrary—may also receive these blessings. Even clearer than the canon is a decree issued recently to the Vicariate Apostolic "*Gabonen*," when the question was asked whether the phrase of canon 1149, "*dari quoque possunt catechumenis*," must be understood, also "*de sacramentalibus publicis ac proinde admitti possint cathecumeni ad impositionem cinerum, traditionem candelarum et palmarum?*" And the reply was in the affirmative.[7]

It is of consequence to note, however, the motive underlying this favor to non-Catholics, "*ad obtinendum fidei lumen vel, una cum illo, corporis sanitatem.*" The primary intention is, therefore, the *lumen fidei*, for "*salvator vult omnes homines salvos fieri et ad veritatis agnitionem venire.*" And the secondary effect may be

5. Schmid, *Die Sakramentalien*, pp. 88-100.
6. Arendt, *De Sacramentalibus*, p. 396.
7. S. R. C. 8 Martii, 1919. A. A. S. XI, 144.

the *corporis sanitatem,* and other temporal favors. "*At vero cum pleraque instituta sint ad removenda gratiae justificantis impedimenta, atque ad praeparandam ipsi viam, dum sacramenta ita exclusive sunt in favorem membrorum Ecclesiae ut primum destinetur ad membrum Ecclesiae inserendum, cetera characterem inserti membri iam exigant: sacramentalia e contra utpote praeparatoria gratiae primae vel catechumenis, vel etiam infidelibus aptari pro sui effectus indole potuerunt.*"[8] Evidently, in these non-Catholics, the dispositions suggested above are not required, at least not in the same degree as they have been there recommended. Nevertheless, a positive averseness to the reception of a benediction, or a vaunted incredulity in the efficacy of the Sacramentals, would not be the most promising disposition under which to administer them to outsiders. "*In istis igitur non requirent fidem actualem tanquam dispositionem nisi ratione obicis removendi vel contrariae incredulitatis vel malae et contrariae voluntatis. Unde continget etiam ut ea Sacramentalia in incredulo vel in gentili efficacia esse possint, quae effectum boni externi temporalis apta sunt perducere: ut energumeni exorcismus saltem ex charismate extraordinario et benedictio quoad bona temporalia: isti sane effectus conducunt ad fidem, sub ratione motive credibilitatis eamque ideo praecedere possunt.*"[9] The minister must, therefore, take due care, and administer benedictions, and the Sacramentals as a whole, only to such as he prudently thinks worthy. He should instruct non-Catholic recipients that they must not look for infallible or even miraculous effects. Furthermore, all superstitious beliefs must be zealously guarded against.[10] In 1768 the Sacred Congregation of the Holy Office allowed priests to visit the

---

8. Arendt, *De Sacramentalibus,* p. 396.

9. Arendt, *op. cit.,* p. 397.

10. Instr. S. C. S. Officii, 11 Dec. 1749 (ad EP. Scorden.) Coll. n. 374.

homes of Turkish families and there bless and pray over the sick *"pro sanitate corporis et pro illuminatione mentis;"* warning them at the same time not to leave with them relics or consecrated objects, especially not if such objects would lead to superstitious practices.[11] But the Sacred Congregation of the Propagation of the Faith allowed priests to bless the homes of Schismatics only when they were summoned by force for this purpose, instructing them to avoid all *"communicatio in oratione."*[12]

The temporal effects of a Sacramental brought to non-Catholics may readily serve to dispose their hearts toward the one true Faith, and hence the liberality of the Church. The fact that she permits benedictions, etc., to be performed over them shows her desire of bringing all men into the fold. She keeps alive the same sentiments that prompted Christ to send His Apostles with the injunction to bless the houses into which they entered, and thus prepare the inmates for the *"Evangelium Christi."*[13] Catechumens can receive the Sacramentals without restriction.[14] Non-Catholics can not receive them all, as the canon provides: *"nisi obstet Ecclesiae prohibitio."* They are positively excluded, for example, from the nuptial blessing. They may be entrusted with blessed objects, like candles, ashes, palms, etc., provided no superstitions will arise, or these objects be exposed to improper uses, or treated disrespectfully. Excommunicated persons and those under personal interdict are forbidden the reception of benedictions and the use of the Sacramentals in general, excepting exorcism, only after a condemnatory or declaratory sentence. As to whether this prohibition affects merely the licitness or also the validity of the Sacramental is a question subject

---

11. S. O. 11 Aug., 1786.
12. S. Congr. de Prop. Fide, 17 Aprilis, 1758, Coll. n. 411.
13. Arendt, *op. cit.*, p. 397.
14. Vermeersch-Creusen, *Epitome* II, p. 248.

to dispute. Since the Sacramentals are controlled exclusively by ecclesiastical law, it might be argued, by way of analogy from canons 2264 and 2266, that *invocative* Sacramentals are invalidly received after a condemnatory or declaratory sentence, but that *constitutive* Sacramentals are forbidden only under pain of illicitness.[15] This argument is no doubt of weight. Nevertheless, since there is question here of an ecclesiastical penalty, canon 2260 must, according to general principles, be interpreted strictly. No mention being made by said canon as to the invalidity of such reception, the milder interpretation would pronounce the reception valid. For practical purposes the latter opinion seems more acceptable.

Per se no one is bound to make use of the Sacramentals, or to receive benedictions, etc. (Abstracting, of course, from those cases where sacramentals accompany other administrations that are of obligation, as, for example, the Sacramentals that accompany the solemn administration of Baptism.) Yet it is the constant desire of the Church that the faithful have a tender and warm attachment to them. For example, the nuptial blessing: "*Parockus curet ut sponsi benedictionem sollemnem accipiant.*"[16] The Holy Office allowed even that absolution could be denied those who refused to receive the blessing.[17] Priests with the *cura animarum* have the obligation, at least *ex caritate,* of properly instructing the faithful regarding the Sacramentals. "*Der Priester versaeume es nicht, im oeffentlichen und Privatunterricht das Volk zu belehren ueber das Wesen, den Gebrauch der Sakramentalien, und ueber die notwendige Disposition.*"[18] "*Usus Sacramentalium nullibi quidem praecipitur, enixe tamen hortandi sunt fideles, ut ea*

15. Canons 2260, 2275, n. 2. Cf. Cappello, *De Censuris,* n. 36.
16. Canon 1101.
17. Ex. Instr. S. C. S. Off. 6 Julii, 1817. Coll. S. C. de prop. Fide, n. 725.
18. Schmid, *op. cit,* p. 108.

frequenter ac devote usurpent ad multiplices eorum effectus percipiendos. Ideo animarum pastores sacramentalium naturam fidelibus exponant, et recto eorum usu eos apte instruant, ut ii, qui sapientiores sibi videntur, ea non contemnant, rudiores vero non superstitioso modo iis utantur."[19]

A distinction is at times, and no doubt properly, made between the recipient and the object of a blessing or consecration. Man alone can be the recipient of a benediction. "*Als Empfaenger aber ist nur der Mensch auzusehen, da auch die Realsegnungen in naeherer oder entfernterer Bezichung zu seiner Heiligung stehen.*"[20] The object may be any created thing, upon which the benedictions of the Church may be performed. By reason of the Fall of our First Parents, the curse of God fell upon all created objects of this world, but by a blessing as indicated before, the curse is removed, at least in part, and the object again elevated to its pristine state.[21] In the blessing of persons, the subject and the object are one and the same, of course, but this fact should not militate against the distinction suggested, albeit, for theoretical rather than for practical reasons.

---

19. Noldin, *op. cit.*, vol. III, p. 60.
20. Amberger, *op. cit.*, III, 1050.
21. Cf. Schmid, *op. cit.*, p. 77.

CHAPTER VI

Reverence Due to Sacred Things

In canon 1150 the Code makes special provisions for the reverence that is due to sacred objects, that is, objects that have been rendered sacred by way of blessing or consecration. Things consecrated or blessed by a constitutive blessing must be treated with reverence. They cannot be used for profane or foreign purposes, although they may be in the possession of private individuals.

These terms of the Code might well serve as a *scholion* or *corollarium* to the canons—and our comment upon them—that have preceded. By a consecration or by a constitutive blessing an object is dedicated to God, and made sacred. "*Semel Deo dicatum, non est ad usus humanos ulterius transferendum.*"[1] Irreverence shown to such an object is practically equivalent to irreverence shown to God. "*Deus autem est objectum cui, seu in cujus injuriam remote actio redundat.*"[2] Disrespect for them falls under the "*actiones irreligiositatis*" and rightly belongs to the class of sacrilege, for sacrilege is nothing else but a "*violatio seu indigna tractatio rei sacrae.*" But a *res sacra* may be said to be "*quidquid ad divinum cultum publicum ritu ex institutione divina vel ecclesiastica deputatur, ideoque specialem reverentiam meretur.*"[3] The greater the sanctity of the object the more heinous the sacrilege.

Now, whereas the *res sacrae* are of three kinds, namely, persons, places and things, authors generally

1. Regula Juris 51 in Sexto.
2. Suarez, *Opera Omnia,* Vol. XIII, p. 601.
3. Sabetti-Barrett, *Theologia Moralis,* p. 222.

conceive three distinct classes of sacrilege, to wit: personal, local and real. "*. . . . et ideo secundum diversam rationem sanctitatis rerum sacrum quibus reverentia exhibetur, necesse est quod sacrilegii species distinguantur. Tanto enim sacrilegium est gravius, quanto res sacra in quam peccatur maiorem obtinet sanctitatem.*"[4]

A. *Reverence Due to Sacred Persons*

A personal sacrilege may be said to be a "*violatio personae sacrae.*" The quality of sacredness in a person may, according to the conception of the canons, be effected in various ways. First of all by the reception of Tonsure (and *a fortiori* by subsequent Orders); secondly, by the public vow of chastity or entry into the religious state, and lastly, by special consecration. Here we are not so much concerned about those persons whose sacred character arises by reason of their vows, or religious profession. These are outside the domain of the Sacramentals. Only those that have received tonsure or consecration or blessing (that is, constitutive blessing) rightly fall under the solicitude of canon 1150. Strange as it may at first sight appear, authors and commentators, as a rule, when treating of sacred persons, fail to take into account those individuals rendered sacred by consecration or blessing. We refer chiefly to consecrated virgins. However, the reason of this may be found in the fact that the blessing of virgins is at the present time not so much in vogue as during earlier eras. But canon 1150, being very general and comprehensive, betrays due anxiety of Holy Mother Church in their favor, and assures them of the reverence and respect which is justly theirs.[5]

Of note at this juncture is canon 119, where all the faithful are advised that they owe the clergy reverence

4. St. Thomas, 2-2 q. 99, a. 3.
5. Cf. Amberger, *Pastoral-Theologie*, III, p. 1112.

according to the rank and office that the clergy enjoy, and that they are guilty of sacrilege if they do them a real injury.[6] The following canons, namely, 120-123, speak of special privileges due to the clergy by reason of their sacred character. Breaches of a serious nature, and worthy of specific condemnation, are the a) *Violenta manuum iniectio.* b) *Usurpatio jurisdictionis, i. e.,* bringing them into secular court, contrary to the *privilegium fori,* or subjecting them to civil *onera* of which, according to the law, they are free. c) *Peccatum luxuriae.* Besides these sacrilegious acts, there are, of course, others that might prove opprobrious to the character of consecrated persons and, though not condemned *nominatim,* fall, however, within the scope of the above named canons. Specific consideration of them should not be necessary here.

B. *Reverence Due to Sacred Places*

By sacred places the Code understands: "All places set aside for divine cult, or burial of the faithful, by way of a consecration or blessing, performed according to the norms of approved liturgy."[7]

Attention need hardly be called here to the numerous decrees and letters extant, calling for due reverence and respect for the sacred places. The zeal of the House of God which animated the patriarch of old and which zeal brought our Divine Saviour to vindicate the rights of the Most High in the Temple of Jerusalem, is beautifully maintained and warmly reflected in the many instructions and legislations that have in the course of epochs emanated from the Holy See,[8] many of which have given rise to and entered into the comprehensive auspices of the present law.

---

6. Cf. c. 29, C. 17, q. 4.
7. Canon 1154.
8. Cf. Annotatio Fontium in Code, under canon 1178.

According to time-honored custom as well as according to the Code now in force, Churches, because of their sacred nature, enjoy first of all *immunity,* by which term is understood: "*Jus competens ecclesiis aliisque locis religiosis vi cuius actus profani, seu saeculares in iis exerceri non valent et malefactores illuc confugientes in vita et membris proteguntur, ita ut extrahi non possint.*"[9] Says canon 1178: "All business transactions, sales, fairs, and in general, everything at variance with the sanctity of the place, shall be kept out of Church, even though the end in view may be a pious one." Contrary to what older theologians teach,[10] the acts chiefly proscribed are:

a) Profane theatrical shows.[11]

b) Profane public gatherings and conventions.[12]

c) Banquets (*convivia*).[13]

d) Seditious gatherings (*seditiosae conclamationes et profanae confabulationes.*[14]

e) Barracks for soldiers.[15]

f) Secular trials, either civil or criminal.[16]

g) Improper music.[17]

h) The use of Churches by Catholics and non-Catholics alike (though tolerated for weighty reasons in some places, *e. g.,* parts of Germany and in the Church of the Holy Sepulchre in Jerusalem). Banners, especially emblems of societies inimical to the Church, must not be

---

9. Coronata, *De Locis et Temporibus Sacris,* p. 39. (quoting Reiffenstuel.)
10. Cf. St. Alphonsus, Tract. III, n. 37.
11. C. 12, X, III, 1.
12. C. 2, III, 23, in VI°.
13. Cl. Trent, Sess. XII, "Quanta Cura."
14. C. 2, III, 23 in VI°.
15. Wernz, *Jus Decretalium,* III, n. 447.
16. C. 5, X, III, 42.
17. Canon 12546, §1.

introduced.[18] A decree of recent date forbids moving pictures and amusements of a kindred type.[19] Pastors that are careless about the demands of this canon 1178 can be proceeded against.[20]

Finally the Church enjoys the *jus asyli,* and criminals may not be taken out without the consent of the ordinary, or at least the rector, unless in case of necessity.[21] The Churches which enjoy this privilege are those that have been consecrated or blessed, as authors generally teach and the text itself betrays. Still, "common jurisprudence would extend it to Churches and public oratories not yet blessed, but dedicated to divine worship. This view may be accepted, as the *ius asyli* is a favor and consequently liable to a broad interpretation."[22] Semi-public and private oratories are not included in this favor. *"Dico autem exclusive quia Codex tantumodo de ecclesiis loquitur; et loca illa supra enumerta excludi videntur, ex eo praesertim quod fere ubique iam ante Codicem contraria consuetudo invaluerat."*[23]

The Code recognizes, furthermore, several acts that not merely offend against the immunity of a sacred place, but rather do actual violence to the sacred character imparted by a benediction or consecration. By the violation of a sacred place is meant the *"temporalis et determinata suspensio effectuum consecrationis aut benedictionis ecclesiae ob quaedam qualificata delicta ibi*

---

18. *"Verum considerandum praeterea est quid ferant iura peculiaria et consuetudines, quae certo possunt plura magis severe excludere. Usus quoque epikeiae non prohibetur. Sic, quod vexillum nationale, quamvis non benedictum afferatur in ecclesiam in functionibus sacris quarum milites sunt participes, id nemo indigne feret vel vetabit."* Vermeersch-Creusen, *Epitome,* II, p. 263.
19. S. C. C. 10 Dec., 1912, AAS, IV, p. 724.
20. Canon 2182-2185.
21. Canon 1179.
22. Augustine, *Commentary,* VI, p. 48.
23. Coronata, *De Locis et Temporibus Sacris,* pp. 45-46.

commissa."[24] A violation does not rob the Church of its consecration or blessing, yet some of the effects of the consecration or blessing, as the lawful celebration of Mass, and sacred offices and ecclesiastical burial are suspended until the Church is reconciled,[25] because of the unbecomingness of celebrating such sacred mysteries in a place defiled by a notorious and public crime.[26]

Four different modes of such violation are recognized.

a) The crime of homicide, which must be *plene imputabilis,* and not due to lawful self-defense or accident. It must be voluntary, even though indirectly.[27] Abortion, if voluntary, is included.[28]

b) Injurious and serious shedding of blood. This shedding must be injurious, by which Vermeersch understands: "*injusta sanguinis effusio.*" Furthermore, the shedding must be serious, or copious, and resulting from a real, serious and imputable harm, inflicted in the Church itself.[29]

c) By being diverted into impious and sordid uses. "*Impious uses*" includes forms of heretical cult, superstitious practices and so forth. Conducting of orgies, Masonic rites, the use of a Church as a place for the execution of criminals.[30] Sordid uses, applies to vile and base purposes, for example, using a Church for barracks, "*ut si convertatur in stabulum, vel in locum quarundem nundinarum.*"[31] It seems to be the spirit of

24. Coronata, *De Locis et Temporibus Sacris,* p. 27.
25. Wernz, Jus Dec. III, n. 442.
26. Coronata, *op. cit.,* p. 27.
27. Suarez, *Opera Omnia,* vol. XIII, p. 385. Vermeersch-Creusen, *Epitome,* II, p. 261.
28. Augustine, *Commentary,* VI, p. 36. Cf. canon 2205. "*Per se, nomine homicidii stricte non venit suicidium. Sed quia ita ferebat superior Codici interpretatio, ex c. 6 hic, quod ad effectum violationis homicidio assimulandum est.*" Vermeersch-Creusen, *Epitome,* II, p. 261.
29. Gasparri, *De SSma Eucharistia,* vol. I, n. 251.
30. Cf. Augustine, *Commentary,* vol. VI, p. 38.
31. Vermeersch-Creusen, *Epitome,* II, p. 261.

the canon, that not a single one of these acts is sufficient for violation, but that a certain use or custom must have arisen. *"Vox usus innuere videtur actionem aliquam singularem quamvis impiam et sordidam, ad hoc non sufficere, sed aliquam consuetudinem seu reptitionem, seu saltem continuationem eiusdem actionis."*[32]

d) By the burial of an infidel or excommunicated person. An infidel in this sense is a person not baptized through his own fault. Heretics and catechumens do not, by being buried, violate a Church, although they are not entitled to Christian burial.[33] Nor do infants that die before baptism, especially if they are born of Catholic parents.[34] Burial of excommunicated persons violates a Church only then, when said person was excommunicated by a condemnatory or declaratory sentence. He need, however, not be a *vitandus*. Persons under suspension or interdict are not included.[35]

The mind of the Church regarding the seriousness of a desecration can best be gathered from canon 1173. In a violated Church it is wrong to hold divine services or to administer the Sacraments or to conduct funeral services, before reconciliation has taken place.[36] If the desecration of the church takes place during divine services, they shall be discontinued at once; if at Mass before the Canon, or after the Communion, Mass is to be

---

32. Coronata, *op. cit.*, p. 28. Cf. S. R. C. 27 Feb., 1847.
33. Cf. Suarez, *Opera Omnia*, XIII, p. 390.
34. Vermeersch-Creusen, *Epitome*, II, p. 262.
35. *"Ecclesia violata ob sepulturam excommunicati vel infidelis ne reconcilietur, antequam cadaver exinde removeatur, si remotio sine grave incommodo fieri possit."* (Canon 1175.) *"Quod si grave habeatur incommodum, tunc remotio cadaveris necessaria non est."* Coronata, *op. cit.*, p. 33.
36. *"Licet haec prohibitio celebrandi officia vel Missam in ecclesia violata per se gravis sit, ut passim docent auctores; si gravis adsit causa, et reconciliatio statim fieri nequeat, Episcopus Missae celebrationem in violata ecclesia permittere potest, vel etiam, si Episcopus interpellari requeat, id rector ecclesiae, in casu verae necessitatis, permittere potest."* Coronata, *op. cit.*, p. 31.

immediately left off, otherwise the priest is to continue until the Communion.[37]

Reconciliation, which is a *"ritus sacer, quo ecclesia violata divino cultui restituitur,"*[38] must take place before services, etc., may be had in a violated Church. In case of doubtful violation canon 1174, §2, says that the Church may be reconciled *ad cautelam*. The reconciliation, in case of a consecrated Church, is to be done by the ordinary of the place, or in case of exempt religious, by the Major Superior. Both can delegate this faculty,[39] and in case of urgent and great need it can even be presumed by the rector of the Church, *certiore facto postea Ordinario*.[40] Under the Old Law simple priests could not reconcile a consecrated Church, except by Apostolic Indult.[41] In case of blessed Churches the rector or any other priest with the permission, at least presumed, of the rector, can perform the reconciliation.[42]

Now, although the Code expressly censures the above named acts, and declares them to be violations of the sanctity, or crimes against the immunity of sacred places, it is not hard to conceive of many other deeds, not mentioned here, that may seriously offend against the reverence due to said places. Wherefore, the appropriateness of canon 1150, which forbids all acts of irreverence, at least as far as the consecrated and blessed Churches are concerned.

The canons relative to the desecration of a Church and its subsequent reconciliation, hold also for the violation and reconciliation of cemeteries.[43]

---

37. *Missale Romanum, de defectibus*, c. X, n. 2.
38. Coronata, *op. cit.*, p. 32.
39. Canon 1176, §2; Canon 1156.
40. Canon 1176, §3.
41. *Rit. Rom.* Tit. VIII, c. 28.
42. Canon 1176, §1.
43. Canon 1203.

C. *Reverence Due to the "Bona Sacra."*

"Bona Sacra" are things destined for divine worship by a consecration or blessing.[44] Chief among these objects are the consecrated and blessed utensils. Regarding these the Code rules that the *"sacra supellex,* especially when blessed or consecrated, according to liturgical law, and destined for public worship, shall be carefully kept in the sacristy of the Church, or in some other safe and decent place, and that they may not be used for profane purposes."[45]

Sacred objects may be desecrated chiefly in three ways, namely, by reducing them to improper uses, by theft and by sale contrary to the indulgence of the Church. Authors on a whole regard it a serious matter to use consecrated objects, specially such as serve most intimately in the celebration of the Divine Mysteries, for secular or profane purposes.[46] Regarding the use, for profane purposes, of objects that are merely blessed, authors are divided, some claiming such deeds to be mortally sinful, whereas others regard them only venially wrong.[47] Should the profane use of sacred vessels proceed from a spirit of contempt, or give rise to scandal, it is not hard to see sufficient matter for grave sin.[48] The Old Law, as to the reduction of sacred vessels to profane uses, was far stricter than the present.[49]

The loss of a consecration or blessing of the *"sacra suppellex"* is effected 1) when the sacred utensils are so badly damaged or so much changed, that they lose their original shape and become unfit for their purpose. As, for example, a serious split in the cup of a chalice,

44. Canon 1497, §2.
45. Canon 1296.
46. Cf. Vermeersch-Creusen, *Epitome,* II, 336.
47. Cf. St. Alphonsus, lib. III, n. 41. D'Annibale, vol. III, n. 16. Vermeersch-Creusen, *Epitome,* II, n. 625.
48. Vermeersch-Creusen, *Epitome,* II, n. 625.
49. Cf. St. Alphonsus, lib. III, n. 41.

or dismembration of vestments, to such an extent that according to ordinary parlance they would be vestments no longer.[50] 2) When they have been used for improper purposes or have been offered on public sale. As improper purposes may be regarded the using of a chalice for drinking cup, or the sacred vestments for festivities, weddings, etc.[51] Vestments and chalices do not lose their sacred character by being used by a *"sacerdos degradatus, vel sectae haereticiae addictus."*[52] Private sale does not rob the *sacra supellex* of its blessing or consecration, but only public sale, as the canon specifies.[53]

The Church's solicitude in the handling of sacred things, is furthermore manifested, when she ordains that the chalices and patens shall be touched by no one except clerics, and those who have the custody of these utensils,[54] abstracting, of course, from cases of necessity. Still, should a lay person touch them, his moral guilt would be only venial.[55] *"Ergo laici religiosi, feminae religiosae, immo etiam saeculares sacristae ipso iure sine speciali facultate illa tangere possunt. Si ab aliis tangantur, veniale non excedit, et si adsit causa, ne veniale quidem est."*[56]

The consecrated oils must be kept under lock and key in a decent and safe place in the Church. Pastors must not keep them in the house except in case of necessity, or for some other reasonable cause, with the consent of the ordinary.[57] They must not, however, be kept in the Tabernacle. A reason admitted by Vermeersch as sufficient for keeping the holy oils in the parochial resi-

---

50. Vermeersch-Creusen, *Epitome,* II, p. 340. Augustine, *Commentary,* VI, p. 285.
51. C. 43, D. 1, de cons.
52. Vermeersch-Creusen, *Epitome,* II, p. 340.
53. Canon 1305, §2.
54. Canon 1306, §1.
55. Sabetti-Barrett, *Comp. Theo. Moralis,* p. 213.
56. Noldin, *op. cit.,* vol. II, p. 197.
57. Canon 735.

dence, would be a great distance between church and parsonage.[58] Canon 946 is somewhat more specific: The *oleum infirmorum* is to be kept by the pastor in a clean and properly ornamented vessel, of silver or white metal, and may not be kept in the house except by reasons given in canon 735.

Blessed and consecrated bells cannot be used for mere secular purposes, except in case of necessity or by the permission of the ordinary, or by reason of lawful custom, prescinding from legitimate stipulations made by the donor with the consent of the ordinary. The use of such bells is regulated exclusively by ecclesiastical authority.[59]

Altars, both immovable and movable, are reserved exclusively for divine services, especially for Mass, and must be secured from all profane use. The burial of corpses beneath the altar is forbidden.[60] An immovable altar cannot be removed from its base, not even for a moment, no matter what necessity may arise, under pain of loss of consecration.[61] Both fixed altars and movable altars lose their consecration by a *fractura enormis*, considered so either because of the fracture itself, or because of the place of the fracture, *i. e.*, the anointed place. Consecration is lost, also, when the relics are removed, or the cover of the sepulchre is broken or removed unlawfully, that is, contrary to canon 1200, §2, n. 2. The desecration of a Church does not carry along with it, the desecration of the altar, either immovable or movable, and *vice versa*.[62]

The reverence due to sacred objects is shown not merely by the canons, but also by the ritualistic prescriptions. Thus, for example, the incensation accom-

---

58. Cf. S. R. C. Dec. 16, 1826.
59. Canon 1169, §3 & 4.
60. Canon 1202.
61. Cf. Canon 1200, §1.
62. Cf. Canon 1200, §§2, 3 & 4.

panying many of the consecrations and blessings, is a mark of reverence: *"Statim vero ac res una benedicta est, donec perduret benedictio, sacra est, et meretur thurificari ob venerationem. Non omnes vero res benedictae thurificari solent, sed illae tantum, quae a Rituali praescribuntur." "Postea Sacerdos genuflexus ante Crucem devote adorat et osculatur et idem faciunt quiqumque voluerint."*[63] *"Deinde Pontifex et successive duodecim Sacerdotes praedicti reverenter salutant oleum ipsum, dicentes tertio in tono lectionis: 'Ave Sanctum oleum.' Et postquam tertio id fecerint, osculantur os ipsius ampullae, prout supra de Chrismate positum est . . ."*[64]

63. *Rit. Rom.* Tit. VIII, c. 24.
64. *Pontificale Romanum, Officio in Feria Quinta Coenae Domini.*

CHAPTER VII

Exorcism—Historical Note—Notion & Division

To complete this study of the Sacramentals, attention must still be called to the doctrine and legislation of the Church on the matter of exorcism. Practically speaking, all authors regard exorcism as belonging to the Sacramentals and forming one class of them. Even the Code makes no exception, but rather places the laws to be observed in the expulsion of evil spirits under the common heading of "*De Sacramentalibus.*"

Exorcism and the Order of Exorcist naturally take for granted the possibility of demoniacal obsession and possession. The materialistic and rationalistic philosophies of the past delightfully scoffed at the belief in the existence of evil spirits and the possibility of their influences upon man. With the advances made, however, in late years, by scientific study in the fields of Spiritism, Spiritualism and Occultism, much of their incredulity has been changed, if not to a positive faith in the demon world, at least to a less glorious form of doubt. For believers in the Sacred Scriptures and Divine Revelation, the possibility of demoniacal possession is a settled matter, so much so that by reason of the Gospel testimonies, the fact of possession and obsession "*citra peccatum haeresis negari non possit.*"

It will be sufficient here to recall the narrative of Job's afflictions to appreciate the teaching of the Fathers and theologians to the effect that through the Fall of Man, the sin of our first parents, Satan gained the mastery over man; but not only over man, but also over the entire world. He became the *princeps huius mundi.*

The entire material universe became subject to him, and his influences were augmented over both man and nature by reason of the curse of Almighty God. "*So ward auch die Erde noch mehr Eigentum des Satans; denn sie ward mit ihm in Fluche vereint, und er konnte dadurch noch mehr auf eine ganz natuerliche Weise auf die Materie, und auf die animalische Seele des Menschen, auf seine Leidenschaften, und dadurch auf den Geist selbst einwirken.*"[1] So clearly have the forces of the unseen spirit world been detectible that of comparatively late years the Council of Trent anathamatized those that would refuse to acknowledge that by the fall of our first parents, man became captive to the *diabolus*.[2]

Christ, by His coming, by His labors, passion and death, redeemed man to a certain extent, indeed, from the woes of Original Sin and the consequent primeval curse. He in fact is said to have conquered Satan, and to have ejected the prince of this world.[3] Nevertheless, our fighting against the principalities and powers has not ceased, but has only been rendered less difficult, by Christ's co-operation. The Devil still goeth about like a roaring lion, seeking whom he may devour. "*Jeder Schuh=Boden muszte ihm mit Gewalt abgerungen werden, und auch jetzt noch, wo Christus seinen Fusz zurueckzieht, da setzt Satan seine Klaune hin.*"[4] His attacks upon poor human nature are in no wise infrequent. By God's permission they may be extremely vehement, and so furious, indeed, that the evil spirit may be said to take possession of us, to control our bodies and through them play havoc upon our souls. St. Thomas, distinguishing between the *potestas impugnandi*, and the *potestas detinendi devictos* of the evil spirit, says: "*Potestatem igitur diaboli, qua victos*

1. Schmid, Die Sakramentalien d. Kath. Kirche, p. 6.
2. Cl. Trent, sess. V, *de peccato Originali*, Denz.-Bann. n. 788.
3. John XII, 31.
4. Schmid, *op. cit.*, p. 7.

detinet, Christus per Passionem ex toto amovit, quantum ad sufficientiam, licet non quantum ad efficientiam, nisi in illis, qui vim Passionis suscipiunt per Fidem, Charitatem, et Sacramenta, et per hoc dicitur dominium diaboli evacuasse. Sed potestatem, qua impugnat, non ex toto evacuavit, sed debilitavit, dum ipsum hostem vicit, et hominibus auxilia multa ad resistendum tribuit, sicut Sacramenta, gratiam abundantiorem, et alia huiusmodi . . ."[5]

The assaults of the Devil upon man, may be of the spiritual order, in the form of temptations, which may arise "*per agentia externa, quae ad peccatum incitant*" or "*ab intrinseco*" "*non quidem efficiendo actum vel speciem vel simile quid in superioribus facultatibus, sed movendo phantasiam per aliquod obiectum vel excitando humores et nervos hominis et generatim proxime influendo in partem inferiorem.*" Or these assaults may be of the physical order, generally known as obsession. Theologians generally recognize three different kinds of obsession. a) Circumsession: "*quando daemon extrinsecus in corpus influit et actiones hominis impedit.*" b) Obsession: "*quando intrinsecus in homine residet et viribus eius physicis tanquam suis utitur, ita ut sit grave internum dissidium inter voluntatem hominis et potestatem daemonis, quia facultates in diversas partes inflectere conantur.*" c) Possession "*si daemon tam plenum dominium obtinet, ut tota fere hominis actio cesset, quamvis daemon numquam directum imperium in voluntatem hominis obtinere possit.*"[6]

Obsession is not a sin, nor necessarily a punishment for sin, but may be permitted by God for good and holy purposes, "*ut ad homines sanctos magis purificandos et simul ad manifestandam malitiam diaboli.*"[7] Never-

5. St. Thos. III, *Sententiarum*, dist. 19, q. 1, a. 2.
6. Pesch, *Praelectiones Dogmaticae*, III, n. 411.
7. Pesch, *op. cit.* III, n. 412.

theless, obsession may readily be favored, perchance induced by a life of sin, for by sinning man forms, as it were, a compact with Satan, Satan may be said to dwell in his heart.[8] St. Cyprian plainly ascribes demoniacal obsession and possession to a life of sin. *"Quam multi quotidie poenitentiam non agentes, nec delicti sui conscientiam confitentes, immundis spiritibus adimplentur, quam multi usque ad insaniam mentis excordes, dementiae furore quatiuntur."*[9]

Before the coming of Christ, the Demons exercised an almost unchecked control over human nature.[10] Paganism frequently was naught but a pure form of demon cult. The wild and weird orgies can best be accounted for and understood under this allowance. With the establishment of Christianity the contest which had been predicted of old began.[11] The homage which Satan had enjoyed for so long a time was not rendered unto him any more by the newly-formed society. His influence over its members was to cease. Wherefore we find him making, as it were, a last and concentrated attack upon the chosen people at the very time when Christ was about to enter upon His public life and inaugurate the long desired reign of peace. *"In der Zeit in welcher sich das Mysterium der Liebe in der Incarnation vollendete, verwirklichte sich zwar das des Hasses in der Obsession am vollstaendigsten."*[12]

Naturally, therefore, faith in Jesus Christ, together with a staunch observance of His law, and a devout practice of the virtues which He counseled and exemplified in His life serve as a general and effective antidote against the wiles and influences of the fallen hosts: *"Je*

8. Orig. Contra Celsum, MPG, XI, 768-770.
9. Cyprian, *de lapsis*, MPL, IV, 487.
10. Cf. Probst, *op. cit.*, p. 40.
11. Orig. in Jesu nat. hom. 14, n. 1, MPG, XII, 892-893.
12. Kirchenlexikon, vol. IV, p. 1142.

mehr die Damonen den Glauben in einem Menschen wachsen sehen, desto mehr weichen sie von ihm zuruck. Von Ihnen aber, welche den vollen Glauben haben fliehen sie ohne Zogern."[13] The Fathers also recommend fastings and prayers as powerful remedies against his assaults. However these means, good and laudable as they may be to protect and defend us in the battle against our common enemy, it is to be feared that in actual cases of obsession they do not apply, inasmuch as the human will and intellect are then seriously hampered in their proper functionings. The condition of the victim of obsession may unfortunately have advanced to such stages, as to make faith and virtue unappreciable quantities for him. Recourse must then be had to different measures, to the special power, namely, which Christ left to the Church in the form of *exorcism.*

Exorcism generally means an "*imperativa adjuratio daemonis.*"[14] The use of the word "*imperativa*" is to call attention to the twofold adjuration generally admitted by theologians. The one is indirect, or *per modum deprecationis,* and is exercised "*per ministerialem collationem auxiliorum gratiae, ad quam revocatur efficacia benedictionis sacerdotalis ac ritus ecclesiae impertoria.*"[15] The other is direct, imperative or *per modum compulsionis,* which St. Thomas explains in the following terms: "*per virtutem Divini Nominis tanquam inimicos repellere, ne nobis noceant spiritualiter, vel corporaliter, secundum potestatem divinam datam a Christo ecce dedi vobis potestatem calcandi supra serpentes, et scorpiones, et supra omnem virtutem inimici et nihil vobis nocebit.*"[16]

Exorcism taken, then, in this sense, "*adjuratio imperativa daemonis,*" did not, strictly speaking, exist

---

13. Probst, *op. cit.,* p. 40.
14. Noldin, *Summa Theo. Moralis,* vol. III, p. 59.
15. Cappello, *De Sacramentis,* vol. I, p. 83.
16. St. Thos. 2-2, q. 90, a. 2.

before the establishment of Christianity. The pagan nations, believing, indeed, in the existence of demons and evil spirits and the possibility of their influences upon man, had apparently many forms of exercises by which they sought to repel the attacks of these spirits; yet their rites consisted chiefly in charms and incantations, as, for example, among the Egyptians; the Babylonians had recourse to the application of medicines and the like. Even among the Chosen People these material means were used,[17] although they also employed certain sacred names and invocations, as we observe from the extra-canonical literature.[18] That their prayers for protection against the powers of darkness were acceptable to God and even answered by Him cannot be denied. Nevertheless, until the coming of Christ we know of no clear-cut case of exorcism from actual obsession. It would appear that during our Lord's public ministry there were certain individuals in Judea endowed with the power of expelling evil spirits. This would seem to follow from the words of Christ Himself: "And if I by Beelzebub cast out devils, by whom do *your children cast them out?*"[19] "John answered him saying, 'Master, we saw one casting out devils in thy name, who followeth not us, and we forbade him.' But Jesus said: 'Do not forbid him. For there is no man that doth miracles in my name and can soon speak ill of me.' "[20] It is probable, then, that even before Christ, or at least at the time of Christ there were certain individuals specially empowered by a charisma to cast out devils, although these two quotations can give rise to only a probable opinion.[21]

---

17. I Kings, XVI, 23. Cf. Smit, *De Daemoniacis,* p. 107.
18. Josephus Archael. l. VIII, c. 2.
19. Matt. XII, 27.
20. Luke IX, 49.
21. Cf. Arendt, *De Sacramentalibus,* p. 344, sqq.

But this question can be of only secondary importance for the present. Far weightier is it to recognize the fact that Christ made use of exorcism in the truest sense of the word. He drove out the evil spirits "*adjuratione imperativa.*" Hardly a page of the Gospels fails to call attention to the unheard-of powers that he exercised over the demon world under the most phenomenal circumstances and conditions. The Pharisees, unable to explain his faculties, attribute them to Beelzebub. But not merely He, even the Apostles and Disciples wrought these same wonders. They receive their powers from him directly and expressly,[22] and exercise them repeatedly. And after the Ascension they faithfully fulfill the prophecy which He left to them on the day of departure, that in His name they should cast out devils.[23] From the Apostles the power passed over to the Christian Community, as countless passages of the early writers testify. We can make room for only a few. Says Origen: "*Haec omnia scient plerique pars vestrum, ipsos daemonas de semetipsis confiteri, quoties a nobis ex tormentis verborum et orationis incendiis de corporibus exiguuntur. Ipse Saturnus et Serapis, et Jupiter, et quidquid daemonum colitis, victi dolore quod sunt eloquitur; nec utique in turpitudinem sui, nonnullis praesertim vestrum assistentibus mentiuntur. Ipsis testibus esse eos daemonas, de se verum confitentibus credite. Adjurati enim per Deum verum et solum, inviti miseris corporibus inhorrescunt, et vel exsiliunt, statim, vel evanescunt gradatim, prout fides patientis adjurat, aut gratia curantis aspirit.*"[24] Justin M. clearly states: "*Per nomen ipsius illius Filii Dei et omnis creaturae primogeniti, qui ex Virgine natus est . . . . daemonium*

22. Matt. X, 1. Mark III, 14.
23. Acts V, 14; VIII, 15; XIX, 16.
24. Minicius Felix, *Octavius*, MPL, III, 325-326.

quodlibet adiuratum vincitur et subicitur."[25] Since the middle of the third century, when the special order of exorcist was established to perform exorcism, testimonies of this nature are so frequent and clear as to render more quotations only odious.

Division of Exorcism

For the purpose of clarifying their comments upon the canons of the Code, authors usually distinguish exorcisms into a) *solemn,* and *simple.* The former is used *"ad expellendos daemones."* The latter *"ad virtutem daemonis compescendam, ne personis vel rebus noceat."* b) *Public*: *"qui fit ab ecclesiae ministris nomine et acutoritate ecclesiae;"* and *private*: *"qui fit proprio nomine exorcizantis."*

25. Justin M, in dial. c. Tryph. MPG, VI, 675.

CHAPTER VIII

MINISTER OF SOLEMN EXORCISM

The prophecy of our Divine Saviour: "In my name they shall cast out devils,"[1] was spoken of all the faithful in general. "These signs shall follow them that believe." Christ foretold that those who should believe in Him should possess the power of exorcising in His name.[2] Now, whether the power here referred to was given to all the believers or only to special ones as a charisma, is not readily determined. The opinion that some of the Christians were specially gifted seems warranted from the quotations of Minicius Felix, where he would have the effect of the exorcism depend on the "*gratia curantis.*" Justine's words lead to the same conclusion: "*Plurimos daemoniis agitatos in toto orbe et in urbe vestra multi ex nostris christianis, cum per nomen Jesu Christi sub Pontio Pilato crucifixi adiurarent, ab omnibus aliis adiuratoribus, incantatoribus et veneficis non sanatos sanaverent, atque nunc adhuc sanant, fractis et eiectis daemonibus homines detinentibus.*"[3] In either case the fact is plain that in the beginning no special ordination or commission was required for the conducting of exorcisms, but the faithful enjoyed this power as a charisma, and even though some may have been more gifted than others, the gift was perhaps denied to no one. "*Usus enim daemonem adiurandi adeo universaliter ab omni fidelium genere et in omni casu occurrente adhibitus exhibetur in documentis mox citandis, ut facilius explicetur huiusmodi frequentia si supponatur non eos solos qui charismate extraordinario fuerant*

1. Mark XVI, 17.
2. Smit, *De Daemoniacis*, p. 86.
3. Justin, *Apologia* II, 6 MPG, VI, 454.

donati, sed fideles quoscumque fide sua sola innixos huiusmodi diaboli obsidentis increpationem usurpasse."[4] The Fathers repeatedly call attention to this singular prerogative of the Christians to prove the divinity of the Christian religion, and its superiority over the pagan cults of those times.[5] And the argument, by reason of the numerous cases of possession of early Christian times, proved, no doubt, of great weight to the well-disposed pagans, who could be prevailed upon in this manner rather than by copious explanation of mysteries and principles to which their minds and hearts had thus far been but faintly educated.[6]

With the gradual spread of Christianity and the firmer hold it obtained on society, the gift of expelling demons seems to have been less generously granted. The number of persons who could exorcise successfully from obsession grew smaller as time advanced. Some places became entirely destitute, and the faithful automatically brought their afflicted to the bishops and ministers of the Church for the purpose of having them delivered from the devil. This course of action gave rise to a certain class of individuals known as the Energumens, or Energumenoi. They lived near the Churches and were subjected to a discipline similar to that in force for the Catechumens. Frequently, however, the Energumens demand special care and attention, since many of them were afflicted not merely with the evil spirits, but were the subject of other physical ailments, that so frequently accompanied actual obsession. The Church literally looked after both their temporal as well as their spiritual needs. A number of ministers or servants

4. Arendt, *De Sacramentalibus,* p. 349. Cf. Tertullian, *Apolog.* c. 23, MPL, I, 413, sqq.
5. Justin M. Apol. I, 40, MPG, VI, 390.
6. "*. . . ad infidelium assensionem ut quibus non persuasit sermo, hos virtus signorum flectat ac pudore afficiat. . . .*" Arendt, *op. cit.,* p. 350.

were, in consequence attached to each Church to take care of the Energumenoi. They were to bring them victuals every day, etc. "*Energumenis in domo Dei adsidentibus victus quotidianis per exorcistas ministretur.*"[7] Furthermore, they had to instruct the Energumens, pray over them and impose hands upon them daily. Thus arose the Office and Order of Exorcist.

As this process was, however, gradual, we look in vain for any early document that *uno ictu* positively forbids the faithful to perform exorcism, or that reserves this function to specially delegated ministers. Nevertheless, at the time of Origen, special regulations were already drawn up to control the performance of exorcism. For example, those conducting the rite were neither to question the demons, nor to address them.[8] Probst's words are in place when he says: "*So weisen solche Vorschriften auf eine ausgebildete Disciplin hin, die das Amt bald nach sich zog, wie dann auch Origenes von foermlichen Exorcisten redet. Die Zeit des Origines bilded darum den Uebergang von der frein Ausuebung des Chrisma zum geregelten Amte.*"[9] At the time of Pope Cornelius (251-252), the office of exorcist was already in operation, for we read in his famous letter to Fabian that in the Roman Church they had then "*Exorcistas et lectores cum ostiariis quinquaginta duos.*"[10] Contrary to the advice of the Constitutions of the Apostles[11] the Council of Laodicea strictly prohibited those who were not ordained exorcists to undertake the deliverance from the evil spirits, even in private.[12] But at the time of the Fourth Synod of Carthage (398), exorcists were specially ordained for their office "The

7. Conc. Carthaginense (IV) c. 90 & 92.
8. Orig. in Matt. XIII, 7, MPG, XIII, 1111.
9. Probst, *Sakramente u. Sakramentalien*, p. 44.
10. Eusebius, *Hist. Eccl.* VI, 43, MPG, 20, 621.
11. Const. Apost. l. VIII, c. 36, MPG, I, 1122.
12. Conc. Laodic. (314) c. 26, MPL, 130, 290.

bishop gives him (the exorcist) the book, saying: 'receive and commit to memory, and possess the power of imposing hands on Energumens, whether baptized or Catechumens.'' In the Greek Church the exorcists were not ordained but merely deputed, because of the lack of minor orders, excepting the Lector, in the Greek Church.

As the practice of infant baptism gained in favor and approval, the number of Catechumens and Energumens was naturally reduced. The fact made the call and office of the exorcist less imperative. Furthermore, from history it appears quite certain that cases of demon obsession grew less and less in number as Christianity gradually supplanted paganism. Abuses, too, seem to have arisen, all of which helped towards the cessation of the faculties which the exorcists at one time enjoyed. Their office was gradually intrusted to higher orders, just as the faculties of deacons and subdeacons have changed remarkably since the early centuries. These changes were, however, very gradual, especially in the western Church.[13]

Under the present discipline no one who has the power of exorcising (by reason of ordination) shall perform the exorcism over possessed persons unless he has received special and explicit permission from the bishop.[14] Incidentally this rule is not new. In fact it can be traced without much effort to remote times,[15] and is taken in good part from the *Rituale Romanum*.[16] To the permission here spoken of all are bound, even exempt religious, though the exorcism is to be conducted in their own house. If, however, the possessed individual belongs to an exempt religious community, the Major Superior can give the permission.[17] The ordinary to

13. Baruffaldo, *Ad Rit. Rom. Commentarium*, vol. II, p. 180.
14. Cf. Catalanus, *Rituale Rom.* Tom. II, p. 301.
15. Rituale Rom. Tit. X.
16. Augustine, *Commentary*, vol. IV, p .569.
17. Vermeersch-Creusen, *Epitome*, II, p. 249.

be approached for the permission is he in whose diocese the exorcism is to take place.[18] For valid procedure this permission from the Ordinary is not required, but only for licit conduct. Nevertheless, because of the scandals that may result, and because of dangers that may accrue to religion if exorcisms are undertaken contrary to the prescriptions of this law, it is conceivable that the law binds *sub grave,* as Cappello mantains.[19] *"Auch ergeben sich durch die Gottlosigkeit einiger Menschen und durch die Leichtglaeubigkeit anderer mancherlei Taeuschungen und Betruegereien, wodurch die heiligen Exorcismen der Kirche dem Gespoette Preis gegeben werden, besonders wenn solche sich finden die aus Eigennutz ganz unbesonnener Weise in das Amt zu exorzisiren sich eindraengen."*[20] No less forceful than the present law are the words of Benedict XIV: *"Ne ullus sacerdos vel saecularis vel regularis exorcizare audeat sive in sua sive in aliena ecclesia, sive intra sive extra coenobium, quin prius a vobis approbatus sit, atque ita ante licentiam a vobis obtinuerit."*[21] Since the Code demands a *"peculiarem et expressam licentiam"* it would be wrong, under ordinary circumstance, to proceed under a presumed or tacit permission. The permission must be *"non factis, sed verbo vel aequipollentibus signis."*[22] It will appear later that this permission is not required for all exorcism, but merely for the *solemn* exorcism of obsessed persons; not for *simple* exorcism of persons or things.

The ordinary is to give this permission, not indiscriminately, but only to priests. Exorcists, though they have in ordination received the power to conduct exorcisms, cannot act licitly under this ruling. Their powers

---

18. Augustine, *op. cit.,* p. 569.
19. Cappello, *De Sacramentis,* vol. I, p. 84.
20. Amberger, *Pastoral-Theologie,* vol. III, p. 1062, quoting Synodalstatuten von Ypern, anno, 1768.
21. Benedict XIV, *ep. encycl. Magno cum,* 2 jun. 1751, §34. Fontes, 413.
22. Blat, *Comment. Text. Cod. J. Canonici,* lib. III, p. 725.

are impeded, both as regards solemn and also simple exorcism.[23] The reason for this restriction can be found in the nature of exorcism itself, which, as was said before, is fraught with dangers of scandal and abuses. Furthermore, great care and thorough acquaintance with the rite are naturally necessary, which qualities may surely be looked for in those advanced in order rather than in those of Minor Orders. The function is likewise reserved *"ob dignitatem adeo eminemtem per quam super Angelos et Daemones evehuntur. Ratio notissima est, quia cum praeter exorcismos, perfici quoque debeant multae benedictiones, cum haec omnia explere nequeat simplex exorcista convenientius fiunt per sacerdotem."*[24] The arguments adduced at one time by certain theologians to the effect that exorcists only should perform the exorcisms, with the idea in mind that this would occasion greater humiliations for the devils than when performed by a priest can, in face of the present law, be of little weight.[25]

The priest selected should be eminent for his piety, prudence and integrity of life, *"eligatur ab Ordinario Sacerdos perspectae pietatis, vitae integritatis atque prudentiae."*[26] The same qualities are demanded by the *Rituale.*[27] *Pietas; ut fidem alteri instillare valeat; prudentia: ut nonnisi quae fieri possunt tenet; vitae integritas: ut Daemon illum redarguere non valeat Evangelico sarcasmo: "Medice cura te ipsum."*[28] The same qualities are equally stressed by the *Pontificale "Studete igitur, ut, sicut a corporibus aliorum daemones expellitis, ita a mentibus, et corporibus vestris omnem immunditiam, et nequitiam ejiciatis; ne illis succumbatis,*

23. Noldin, *op. cit.*, vol. III, p. 59.
24. Baruffaldo, *op cit.*, vol. II, p. 181.
25. Catalanus, *op. cit.*, Tom. II, p. 300.
26. Canon 1151.
27. Rit. Rom. Tit. X.
28. Baruffaldo, *op. cit.*, vol. II, p. 182.

quos ab aliis, vestro ministerio, effugatis. Discite per officium vestrum vitiis imperare; ne in moribus vestris aliquid sui juris inimicus valeat vindicare. Tunc etenim recte in aliis daemonibus imperabitis, cum prius in vobis eorum multimodam nequitiam superatis."[29] Besides these marks the minister of exorcism is to have purity of intention, as called for by the prescription of the *Rituale*: "*non sua, sed divina fretus virtute, ab omni rerum humanarum cupiditate alienus, tam pium opus ex caritate constanter et humiliter exequatur.*"[30] He is to pronounce the exorcism freely, not seeking material recompense.[31] Finally the minister should be of mature years.[32] However, these qualities must not be stressed so heavily as to create the impression that the effects sought by the exorcism depend entirely upon the *opus operantis*. This notion would be wrong. The priest, when pronouncing exorcisms, labors in the name of the Church and as a minister of the Church. So that, even though he were not eminent for his piety, prudence or integrity of life, the exorcism would nevertheless produce its effects. Actual liberation from the evil spirit may not take place, for, as has been said before, the invocative Sacramentals do not produce the "desired" or "determined" effect infallibly. "*Exorcismus rite prolatus etiam a sacerdote aut ab episcopo, non habet infallibilem effectum, saltem completum, i. e., omnimodam eiectionem diaboli ex homine obsesso. Quare verba S. Scripturae: 'Signa eos, qui crediderint, haec sequentur: in nomine meo daemonia eicient, linguis loquentur novis,' non significant, omnes credentes valere semper et statim eicere daemones, sed quando Evangelii profectus id postulaverit; sicuti nec etiam omnes credentes semper possunt loqui linguis novis. Nihilominus cum*

29. *Pontificale Rom. De Ordinatione Exorcistarum.*
30. Rituale Rom. Tit. X. c. 1.
31. Laymann, *Theo. Moralis,* Tom. II, p. 383.
32. Rit Rom. et *Baruffaldo, op cit.*, et l. cit.

S. Alphonso et compluribus aliis auctoribus oportet admittere, exorcismum a clerico insignito ordine exorcistatus prolatum producere ex opere operato saltem attenuationem virium daemonis obsidentis."[33]

Before the priest proceeds to pronounce exorcism, he must by diligent and prudent investigation determine whether the person to be exorcised is really obsessed. Frequently the final decision as to whether public and solemn exorcism is to be actually undertaken or not, is to be left to the bishop.[34] In Christian countries cases of actual obsession and especially of possession are comparatively rare. Among the pagan nations they occur more frequently.[35] Many types of sicknesses, especially mental sicknesses, may closely resemble, in their symptoms, demoniacal obsession. Hence the Code demands prudence on the part of the minister, so that he may not be too easily persuaded that individuals manifesting these symptoms are in reality under demoniacal control. Apropos is the remark of Baruffaldo: "*Si omnes illi qui daemoniaco morbo se laborare dicunt, vere daemoniaci essent, pene totus orbis esset a daemone obsessu et praecipue totus foeminarum grex . . . .*"[36] The danger of deceptions being practiced in this respect has long been recognized. Wherefore we find special punishments enacted against the perpetrators of these deceptions. The Fathers of the Trullan Council of 692 drew up the following: "*Eos, qui se a daemone correptos esse simulant, et morum improbitate eorum figuram, et habitum simulate praeseferunt, visum est omnimodo puniri, et ejusmodi afflictionibus, laboribusque eos subjici oportere, quibus ii, qui vere a daemone correpti sunt, ut a daemonis operatione liberentur, jure subjiciuntur.*"[37]

33. Pruemmer, *Man. Theo. Moralis,* Tom. II, p. 375.
34. Pruemmer, *op. cit.,* Tom. II, p. 463.
35. Cf. Nevius, *Demon Possession and Allied Themes.*
36. Baruffaldo, *op. cit.,* vol. II, p. 182.
37. Conc. Trull. can. 60. Cf. Catalanus, op. c. p. 303.

To obtain certitude, at least moral certitude, in this respect, some authors advise that men experienced in medicine and pathology be first consulted. The Code itself would not impose this, nor the *Rituale.* Yet particular injunctions to this effect are not wanting. Of interest is one such law given by Amberger: "*Nulli in posterum exorcizandi facultatem nos concessuros declaramus nisi sub attestatione in scriptis a pastore loci nobis exhibita, quo fidem faciat ex signis, suo, medicorum aliorumque prudenti judicio examinatis, moraliter constare de daemonum infestatione aut incantationum maleficiis.*[38] But even though the testimony and opinion of men experienced in medicine and pathology were obtained, the minister, nevertheless, would have to conduct his own diligent examinations and studies of the one to be exorcised. In his observations special attention should be directed to the signs which the Roman Ritual and authors of recognized authority set down as acceptable indications of obsession or possession. Among these signs the *Rituale* mentions: the fluent use and knowledge of a strange tongue, the unearthing of distant and unknown things; revelation of powers surpassing the age and natural accomplishments of the subject, "*et id genus alia, quae cum plurima concurrunt, majora sunt indicia,*" Ferraris gives a number of other signs, that may serve as indications of demon control. In themselves these signs furnish no absolute proof, but are only indications. The degree of moral certitude of possession will depend upon the actual value and number of these indications. For it is a well-known fact that many of the Saints made themselves responsible for "signs and wonders." But, as St. Augustine says: "*Cum talia faciunt magi, qualia sancti, diverso fine et diverso iure fiunt. Illi enim faciunt quaerentes gloriam suam, iste*

38. Amberger, *op. cit.*, vol. III, p. 1063, quoting the Pastoralinstruktion Von Yporn, c. 156.

quaerentes gloriam Dei; et illi faciunt per quaedam privata commercia, isti autem publica administratione, et iussu Dei, cui cuncta subiecta sunt."[39]

To confirm the minister's opinion still more, the *Rituale* says: "*post unum aut alterum exorcismum interrogat obsessum, quid senserit in animo, vel in corpore, ut sciat etiam, ad quaenam verba magis diaboli conturbentur, ut ea deinceps magis inculcet ac repetat.*"[40] Some words seem to be especially offensive to the demons, and as exorcists have experienced, the evil spirits are greatly perturbed by them. Says Baruffaldo: "*quamvis enim nulla verba vim habeant naturalem aliquid efficiendi more agentis physici, attamen sunt quaedam verba, quae habent vim operandi ex institutione Dei, et eorum effectus est supernaturalis.*"[41] To which the words of St. Cyprian might be added: "*O si audire eos velles, et videre, quando a nobis adjurantur, et torquentur spiritualibus flagris, et verborum tormentis de obsessis corporibus ejiciuntur, quando ejulantes, et gementes voce humana, et potestate divina flagella et verbera sentientes venturum Judicium confitentur.*"[42]

Once the fact of possession has been prudently concluded upon and appears morally certain, the priest is to study closely and thoroughly the *modus procedendi*, as given by approved sources. Great harm may be done to the cause of religion and to both exorcist and victim, if the exorcism is ventured upon ignorantly or rashly. "*Wenn diese Gewalt von Unvorsichtigen und Unklugen, welche in Handhabung der geistlichen Waffen unerfahren sind, unbesonnener Weise ausgeuebt wird, entsteht bei den Glaeubigen nicht gerings Aergerniss, bei den Unglaeubigen aber Verachtung der heiligen Gebraeuche und*

---

39. St. Augustine, *De Divinatione Daemonum*, MPL, XL, 586.
40. Rit. Rom. Tit. X, c. 1, n. 4.
41. Baruffaldo, *Ad Rit. Rom. Comment.* vol. II, p. 184.
42. St. Cyprian, *Ad Demetrianum*, MPL, IV, 555.

Ceremonien der Kirche."[43] The *Rituale* warns, therefore, to the effect that the demons will use every possible art of deception, so as to put even the prudent and skilled exorcist to the test. They will reveal themselves only reluctantly "*ut Exorcista diu defatigatus desistat; aut infirmus videatur non esse a daemonio vexatus.*"[44] Says St. Augustine: "*Fallunt autem etiam studio fallendi, et invida voluntate, qua hominum errore laetantur.*"[45] As a general rule the exorcist must not believe the responses of the "*pater mendacii,*" and he is not to desist in the exorcism until definite proofs are at hand that the devil has been expelled. For as the *Rituale* admonishes, "*aliquando postquam sunt manifesti, abscondunt se, et relinquunt corpus quasi liberum ab omni molestia, ut infirmus putet se omnino esse liberatum.*"[46] "*Aliquando etiam daemones ponunt quaecumque possunt impedimenta, ne infirmus se subjiciat exorcismis, vel conantur persuadere infirmitatem esse naturalem.*" Frequently physical sickness and demoniacal possession go hand in hand. "Lord have pity on my son, for he is a lunatic, and suffereth much . . . ." In case of a doubt, which cannot otherwise be settled, authors recommend that the exorcist command the evil spirit to reveal himself. A few other modes of deception commonly practiced by the demons are given by the *Rituale*: "*interdum in medio exorcismi faciunt dormire infirmum, et ei visionem aliquam ostendunt, subtrahendo se, ut infirmus liberatus videatur. Aliqui ostendunt factum maleficium, et a quibus sit factum, et modum ad illud dissipandum: sed caveat, ne ob hoc ad magos, vel ad sagas, vel ad alios, quam ad ecclesiae ministros confugiat, aut ulla superstitione, aut alio modo illicito utatur. Quandoque diabolus*

---

43. Amberger, *op. cit.*, vol. III, p. 1062, quoting Dioezesansynode von Muenster, anno 1752.
44. Rit. Rom. Tit. X, c. 1, n. 5.
45. St. Augustine: *De Divinatione Daemonum*, MPL, XL, 587.
46. Rit. Rom. Tit. X, c. 1, n. 6.

infirmum quiescere, et suscipere sanctissimam Eucharistiam permittit, ut discessisse videatur. Denique innumerabiles sunt artes et fraudes diaboli ad decipiendum hominem, quibus ne fallatur, Exorcista cautus esse debet."[47]

Nor must the spiritual preparation of the minister be in any way neglected. A strong and lively faith is indispensable. "*. . . je mehr die Daemonen den Glauben in einem Menschen wachsen sehen, desto mehr weichen sie von ihm zurueck. Von Jenen aber, welche den vollen Glauben haben, fliehen sie ohne Zoegern.*"[48] The failure of the disciples, spoken of in Matt. XVII, was due to their unbelief. The exorcist is given the advice to proceed only after a worthy confession, or at least a heartfelt contrition, and after having said Mass, if convenient, and devoutly implored the Divine help. The success of exorcism depends perchance upon the disposition of both minister and subject more than do the effects of the other Sacramentals, because of the fact that exorcism is generally looked upon as a battle, or contest, in which the Church is ultimately to triumph.[49] The worthy celebration of Mass is much to be counseled.[50] "*Tum confessus, conscientia ab omni culpa pura, ac munda, magna cum humilitate, et fide, memor potestatis, quam a Domino accepit expellendi daemones, ad id munus obeundum accedat.*"[51] At times, however, these ordinary preparations are not enough. Some demons are cast out but by prayer and fasting. This is a fact emphasized by the Scriptures and well-recognized by the early Christians.[52] Instances of protracted obsession were customarily regarded as harder of cure. The fasting counseled by

47. Rit. Rom. Tit. X, c. 1, nn. 7, 8 & 9.
48. Probst, *op. cit.*, p. 40.
49. Goerres, *Christliche Mystik*, IV, p. 301.
50. Augustine, *De Civitate Dei*, l. 22, c. 8.
51. Catalanus, *Rit. Rom. Tom.* II, p. 302, quoting St. Charles.
52. Const. Apost. l. VIII, c. 7.

the *Rituale*, though advisable for both minister and subject, applies primarily to the priest, as is also clear from the seventeenth chapter of Matthew's Gospel. The duration of the fast and prayer will naturally depend upon the nature of the case. St. Charles advises: "*Pridie illius diei, quo alicui exorcismum adhibere incoeperit, se jejunio, et oratione praeparare studeat.*"[53] The importance of the proper preparation was familiar in remotest times. St. Iraeneus says: "*Nec invocationibus angelicis facit aliquid, nec incantationibus, nec reliqua prava curiositate, sed munde et pure et manifeste orationes dirigens ad Dominum, qui omnia fecit et nomen Domini Nostri Jesu Christi invocans, virtutem ad utilitates hominum sed non ad seductionem perfecti.*"[54]

53. Baruffaldo, *op. cit.*, II, p. 188.
54. Iren. l. 2, c. 32, n. 5, MPG, VII, 830.

CHAPTER IX

The Rite of Éxorcism

The mode of procedure in the expulsion of demons has hardly changed since the third century.[1] The ceremony is properly divided into three parts. The first part serves as a general preparation and consists in the recitation of the Litany of the Saints and some special prayers. Next comes the immediate preparation of the minister and subject. The Church's power over the demon world is declared. Passages from the Gospels are read, especially such as treat of Christ's powers over the evil spirits. Lastly we have the actual imperative adjuration, in the name of God or in the name of Jesus Christ.

At the time of St. Athanasius certain exorcists proceeded without the lessons from the Sacred Writ: "*Quare omni damnatione dignos esse dicebat eos qui, his omissis adscitisque aliunde verbis elegantibus in iis sese exorcistas nominarent. Potius enim ludunt ac se daemonibus ridendos offerunt, sicut accidit Judais filiis Scevae, qui eo ipso modo exorcizare tentaverunt.*"[2] All exorcisms are conducted in the name of God or in the name of Christ. "*Adjurati enim per Deum verum et solum, inviti, miseri, corporibus inhorrescunt.*"[3] The reason of this is, that the demons are subject to God alone, and hence can be forced by him alone to obey. They are not subject to man, as man, not even to the ministers of the Church. "And the seventy-two returned with joy, saying: Lord, the devils also are subject to us, *in thy name.*"[4] "*Daemones Christum timentes in Deo*

1. Cf. Probst, *Sakramente u. Sakramentalien*, p. 52.
2. St. Athanasius, *ad Marcellinum*, MPG, XXVII, p. 46.
3. Min. Felix, *Octav.* c. 27, MPL, III, p. 326.
4. Luke, X, 17.

et Deum in Christo, subjiciuntur servis Dei et Christi."[5] Chrysostom asserts that the demons are afraid of the Sacred Names and flee at the mere sound of them.[6] The prayers pronounced in exorcism are accompanied by certain symbolical actions as contact, "*insufflatio*" and "*exsufflatio,*" etc. "*Ita de contactu deque afflatu nostro, contemplatione et repraesentatione ignis illius correpti, etiam de corporibus nostro imperio excedunt inviti et dolentes, et vobis praesentibus erubescentes.*"[7] The sign of the cross and the imposition of hands is most common. The demons tremble at the sign of the cross and the first Christians at times used nothing more for the expulsion.[8]

The ceremony itself is to take place in Church, when this is possible. By ancient custom the Energumens were brought to Church and there the bishop, frequently during public service, pronounced the exorcism,[9] although this practice was not uniform. Where a Church cannot be had conveniently, the exorcism may be conducted in another place of a religious and respectable nature, but always away from the multitude. Some authors advocate that a private oratory or at least, a Church where curious spectators will not be attracted, be chosen, in preference to a much frequented sacred edifice.[10] For a just cause, as, for example, in the case of sickness, or in case of the nobility, and also other just causes, the ceremony may take place in private homes, observing, of course, the prescribed regulations.[11]

---

5. Tertullian, Apol. c. 23, MPL, I, p. 415.
6. Chrysost. *De Laudibus Pauli Hom.* 4.
   "*Daemones naturaliter horrent mysteria fidei, quibus se victos esse sciunt; ideo viso signo crucis et audito nomine Jesu, aliisque similibus torquentur et fugiunt.*" Pesch, *op. cit.*, VI, n. 342.
7. Tertullian, Apol. c. 23, MPL, I, 415.
8. Cyril H. MPG, XXXIII, p. 774.
9. Cf. Kraus, Real-Encyclopaedie.
10. Baruffaldo, *op. cit.*, vol. II, p. 189.
11. Rit. Rom. Tit. X, c. 1, n. 11. Cf. Catalanus, *op. cit.*, Tom. II, p. 313.

Neither the *Rituale* nor the Canon Law prescribe anything as to the time when exorcism should be undertaken.[12]

During the exorcism of obsessed persons the minister must not engage in idle talk, or propose vain or curious questions, especially concerning future and occult things.[13] Under such circumstances the proper devotion bespeaking the seriousness of the undertaking could hardly be had. "*Si enim Daemon cognoscat Exorcistae verbositatem, novas occasiones loquendi suppeditabit, et sic distrahet illum a munere suo recte fungendo, et consequenter dominium illius habebit,*"[14] He is rather to proceed seriously and enjoin the necessary silence upon the demon, in conformity to our Lord's example,[15] only allowing the evil spirit to reply to the questions proposed. Nor should the minister give credence to the demon when he claims to be the spirit of a Saint, or a deceased, or an angel.[16] Instances of this nature we find in the life of St. Catherine, to whom the devil appeared in the form of Christ crucified.[17]

However, all questioning cannot be avoided, nor are prudent interrogations, pertaining to the function proscribed by the Church. The Ritual allows the minister certain freedom in this respect. "*Necessariae vero interrogationes sunt, ut de numero et nomine spirituum obsidentium, de tempore quo ingressi sunt, de causa, et aliis hujusmodi. Ceteras autem daemonis nugas, risus, et ineptias Exorcista cohibeat, aut contemnat, et circumstantes, qui pauci esse debent, admoneat, ne haec curent, neque ipsi interrogent obsessum, sed potius humiliter et*

12. Cf. Baruffaldo, *op. cit.*, vol. II, p. 189.
13. Rit. Rom. Tit. X, c. 1, n. 14.
14. Catalanus, *op. cit.*, Tom. II, p. 316.
15. Luke IV, 35; Mark I, 34.
16. Rit. Rom. Tit. X, c. 1, n. 14.
17. Cf. II. Corinth. XI, 14; Baruffaldo, *op. cit.*, vol. II, p. 192 St. Thos. I. Quest. 117, a. 4, n. 2.

enixe Deum pro eo precentur."[18] The information so received is, however, very unreliable and necessarily unsatisfactory. By adjuring the evil spirit to give his name, number, etc., more trustworthy statements may be expected. Nevertheless, it must be borne in mind that the evil spirit is the "*Pater Mendacii.*" Above all will he try to deceive the exorcist, who attempts to expel him. Wherefore it can be expected that he will give fictitious names, ridiculous names, even vulgar and improper names. "*Atque ideo quamvis rituale necessarias ducat has interrogationes, et non omittendas; attamen quia praxis in contrarium docet, possunt omitti quia pessimos fructus gignunt.*"[19]

The form of adjuration, or the exorcism proper, is to be read in a dignified manner, with authority, as also with a strong faith, with humility and fervor.[20] For this reason some older writers recommend that the minister commit the form of exorcism to memory. Baruffaldo interprets the words of the Ritual thusly: *Aspere igitur, cum tanto hoste loquatur, dulces sermones omnino coerceat, et reprimat.*"[21] Should the evil spirit seem to be greatly troubled, the minister is to repeat the words of exorcism frequently. He should have to hand Holy Water, and should sprinkle the victim and also himself, when special signs or manifestations of the evil spirit appear. "*Et quoties viderit obsessum in aliqua corporis parte commoveri, aut pungi, aut tumores alicubi apparere, ibi faciat signum crucis, et aqua benedicta aspergat, quam exorcizando in promptu habeat.*"[22] Physical deformities or special pains, etc., should not be

---

18. Rit. Rom. Tit. X, c. 1, n. 15.
19. Baruffaldo, *op. cit.*, vol. II, p. 193. St. Thos. I, 2 Quest. 89, a. 4, n. 3.
20. Mark IX, 24. Rit. Rom. 1 c. n. 16.
21. Baruffaldo, *op. cit.*, vol. II, p. 194.
22. Rit. Rom. l. c. n. 16.

dispelled by recourse to medical means, since they are not signs of natural infirmities.[23]

The forms of threat (*comminationes*) should be repeated several times. "*Quando pervenerit ad comminationem, eam iterum et saepius proferat, semper poenam augendo; ac si videat se proficere, in ipsa perseveret per duas, tres, quatuor horas, et amplius prout poterit, donec victoriam consequatur.*"[24] "*Fateor,*" says Baruffaldo, "*quidem, longus, et inexplicabilis labor est, sed non sine longo certamine reportatur victoria: nihilominus haberi debet ratio etia mad vires corporales exorcistae, quae, adeo defatigari non debent, ut langueat, et ad operas necessarias inutilis reddatur, et pereat.*"[25]

In case the exorcism prove unsuccessful, the minister is to pray the more ardently and prepare himself the more zealously by prayer and fastings, etc. He should persist until he observes signs of deliverance.[26] The nature of these signs will vary, probably, with each case, and writers generally acknowledge that no sign can be regarded as an infallible indication that the demon has actually departed. The cessation of the indications of possession previously referred to, may perchance be safe signs of the success of the exorcism. Still, the study of each individual case, each patient, as well as actual experience will no doubt be of greater service to the minister in determining the results of his ministrations, than authors can hope to suggest.

---

23. Rit. Rom. l. c. n. 18. "*Caveat proinde Exorcista, ne ullam medicinam infirmo obsesso praebeat, aut suadeat; sed hanc curam medicis relinquat.*
24. Rit. Rom. l. cit. n. 17.
25. Baruffaldo, *op. cit.*, vol. II, p. 195.
26. "*Nec debet Sacerdos opus suum relaxare, sed magis, ac magis insistere et vires omnes, renovare, ut tandem inimicus taedio affectus extruadatur omnino.*" Baruffaldo, *op. cit.*, vol. II, p. 185.

CHAPTER X

THE SUBJECT OF SOLEMN EXORCISM

From the Gospels it is clear that Christ pronounced exorcism not merely over those who might be called his followers or disciples, but even over others. So the Church, too, allows exorcism in favor of not only the faithful, but also in favor of catechumens, non-Catholics and even excommunicated persons.[1] This is not a new concession of the present law. We know that St. Paul liberated the girl of her pythonic spirit, as is narrated in the Acts.[2] Since the Code uses the term, "*sed etiam in excommunicatos,*" it would seem that not even the *vitandi* are forbidden to receive the exorcism, although they cannot receive the other Sacramentals. Excommunication, being a medicinal remedy, could hardly be expected to achieve its purpose in a subject under the influence of the evil spirit.[3]

In order to achieve the desired effect in the exorcism, the minister should attempt to properly dispose the subject, where this can be done. The preparation of the obsessed consists in prayers, fastings and frequent reception of the Sacraments, according to the prudent judgment of the minister. The advisability of prayers and fasts is clear, from the seventeenth chapter of St. Matthew. Since obsession in many cases is due to a life of sin, the necessity of removing sin through Sacramental absolution can hardly be questioned. Says St. Charles: "*Energumenis Exorcismum ne adhibere incipiat, nisi illi primum confessi sint; ad hocque eos*

1. Canon 1152.
2. Acts XVI, 16-18.
3. Cf. Vermeersch-Creusen, *Epitome,* II, p. 249.

cohortetur, ut omnis anteactae vitae peccata diligenti conscientiae discussione confiteantur."[4] The reception of Holy Communion was at one time strictly forbidden to the Energumens, "*nisi in ultima vitae periodo.*" Later on this discipline was modified so that those obsessed individuals that had lucid intervals could receive at that time.[5] The reception of Holy Communion is now left to the prudent judgment of the minister of the exorcism, who naturally will be guided by the principles laid down in approved works of theology. During the act of exorcism the subject is to be recollected, having his heart and mind raised to God and confidently and humbly await help from Him, not distrusting, even though the evil spirit trouble him exceedingly.[6] For, as has been said before, faith and confidence are of the utmost import: "*Daemones vel exiliunt statim, vel evanescunt gradatim, prout fides patientis adjuvat, aut gratia curantis aspirat.*" The obsessed person is to hold in hand, or have before his eyes, a crucifix. Where relics of the Saints can be had, being decently and safely guarded and covered, they should be reverently brought near the obsessed person, "*ad pectus, vel ad caput.*" During this ceremony due care must be taken that the relics are properly handled and no irreverence be done to them, through the influences of the Devil.[7] "*Eo quia sicuti, viventibus Sanctis, daemones eorum hostes fuere, ita et post mortem eorum nominibus sunt infensi, multoque magis eorum exuviis, quarum tactu torquentur, clamant, infremunt, nec quiescere possunt; imo tentant eas contemnere, et conculcare sed ad consummandum actum non valent . . . .*"[8] Which fact will counsel due care on the part of the exorcist. Instances are on record

---

4. Catalanus, *Rit. Rom.* Tom. II, p. 314, quoting St. Charles.
5. Catalanus, *op. cit.*, Tom II, p. 311.
6. Cf. Catalanus, *op. cit.*, Tom. II, p. 315.
7. Rit. Rom. l. c. n. 13.
8. Baruffaldo, *op. cit.*, vol. II, p. 191.

where, instead of the relics, the Blessed Sacrament was employed for this ceremony.[9] Due to the danger of irreverence, the Blessed Sacrament must not be placed "*super caput obsessi, aut aliter ejus corpori admoveatur.*"[10]

When the possessed or obsessed person is a woman, the minister is to employ persons of upright character, who are to sustain her during the exorcism. The persons called upon to help the exorcist should, if possible, be close relatives of the possessed. During the exorcism the priest is to be careful: "*ne quid dicat, vel faciat, quod sibi, aut aliis occasio esse possit pravae cogitationis.*"[11]

After a successful exorcism, the *Rituale* prescribes that the minister instruct the patient to carefully avoid sin, lest he offer the demon an opportunity of reentering and thus have his last condition prove worse than the first.[12] *Dicitur tamen (Diabolus) inhabitare affectum hominis per effectum malitiae, non solum quando eius suggestione peccatum perpetratur, sed etiam per quodcumque peccatum mortale; quia ex quocumque peccato mortali homo servituti diaboli addicitur.*"[13] If the first obsession was due to a sinful life, at least indirectly, the patient must avoid especially those sins which brought on the affliction. Authors agree that a second expulsion will be harder than the first, because of the lack of proper dispositions on the part of the subject, as no doubt the Scriptural words alluded to imply. "Then he goeth, and taketh with him seven other spirits more wicked than himself, and they enter in and dwell there, and the last state of that man is made worse than the first."[14]

9. Cf. Catalanus, *op. cit.,* Tom. II, p. 191.
10. Rit. Rom. l. cit. n. 13.
11. Rit. Rom. l. cit. n. 19.
12. Rit. Rom. l. cit. n. 21.
13. Cf. Arendt, *op. cit.*, p. 59.
14. Matt. XII, 45.

CHAPTER XI

Simple Exorcism

Simple exorcism, as stated before, is the "*adjuratio imperativa*" performed "*ad virtutem Daemonis compescendam, ne personis vel rebus noceat.*" It is distinguished from solemn exorcism, inasmuch as it, generally speaking, serves not in cases of actual obsession or possession, but is used rather against the wiles of the demons, who through the Fall of Man and the curse of Almighty God, gained such a powerful hold upon man and all nature.[1]

Simple exorcism, as an ecclesiastical practice and Sacramental, seems to have originated somewhat later than the solemn exorcism of obsessed persons.[2] The first uses undoubtedly centered around the administration of the Sacrament of Baptism. It was used very early, in the blessing of Baptismal Water. And at the time of Tertullian the renunciation of Satan by the Catechumens was already practiced. Later on, probably during the fourth century, this renunciation was followed by the exorcism, as we have it today in the administration of solemn baptism.[3]

Minister of Simple Exorcism

The exorcisms that occur in baptism and in consecrations and blessings, may be performed by those who

1. *Nam etsi omnes creaturae Dei bonae sint, non ignoramus tamen, daemonem his ipsis saluti et incolumitati nostrae insidias struere posse; quam ob causam ex pervetusto Ecclesiae ritu ante usum illas benedicimus: ad quam benedictionem ipse exorcismus refertur, ut si forte daemon in usu illius creaturae nobis nocumentum pararet, exorcismo seu adjuratione compulsus discedat.*" De Herdt, *Sacrae Lit. Praxis*, III, p. 183.
2. Cf. Augusti, *Christliche Archaeologie*, vol. II, p. 429.
3. Cf. Probst, *Sakramente u. Sakramentalien*, p. 132.
4. Canon 1153.

are the lawful ministers of these sacred rites.[4] No special permission or delegation is, therefore, necessary. Exorcists not having the power to conduct blessings and consecrations or to administer solemn baptism, are, by way of exclusion, forbidden to exercise the power of their order. Deacons, as the extra-ordinary ministers of solemn baptism, can pronounce the exorcism over the subject to be baptized. Priests again, by way of elimination, cannot perform the exorcisms that are employed in consecrations, unless they have received special faculties to consecrate.

The effects of simple exorcism, both spiritual and temporal, can be deduced from what has been said above on the Sacramentals in general. Worthy of special note is a letter directed to the Holy Office, under date of 17 Sept., 1681, by missionaries of Scotland, wherein it is maintained that obsessed individuals, who had been validly baptized as non-Catholics, were freed from the vexations of the evil spirit, when the ceremonies of solemn baptism were supplied. "*Quibus* (*caeremoniis*) *suppletis, saepe dicti obsessi et possessi a molestiis et vexationibus dictis liberantur ct remanent immunes, et magna quiete reliquum vitae degere solent* . . . ."[5] In most of these cases solemn exorcism had proven ineffective. Hence the words of Noldin seem in place: "*Valde suadendum est ecclesiae ministris, ut exorcismum simplicem saepius peragant memores verbi domini: in nomine meo daemonia eiicient; praesertim vero super eos, qui vehementi tentatione vexantur, et super poenitentes, quos advertunt difficultates experiri in eliciendo dolore et proposito de peccatis vel in peccatis suis sincere manifestandis. Uti possunt hae vel simili formula: In nomine Jesu praecipio tibi, spiritus immunde, ut recedas ab hac creatura Dei.*"[6]

5. S. C. S. Officii, 17 Sept. 1681, Collectanea, 225.
6. Noldin, *op. cit.*, III, p. 61.

BIBLIOGRAPHY

Amberger, Joseph, *Pastoraltheologie*, Regensburg, 1866.

Arendt, Guillelmo, *De Sacramentalibus—Disquisitio Scholastico—Dogmatica*, Romae, 1900.

Arregui, Antonius M., S. J., *Summarium Theologiae Moralis*, Ed. Eluspuru Hnos. (Bilbao), 1919.

Augusti, D. Johann Christian, *Handbuch der Christlichen Archaeologie*, Leipzig, 1836.

Augustine, Chas., O. S. B., *A Commentary on the New Code of Canon Law*, St. Louis, 1922.

Ballerini, Antonius, S. J., *Opus Theologicum Morale edidit Palmieri, S. J., Prati*, 1891.

Baruffaldo, Hieronymus, *Ad Rituale Romanum Commentaria*, Florentiae, 1847.

Bellarminus, Robertus, *Opera Omnia*, Vol. III, Neapoli, 1872.

Berti, J. Laurentius, *Opus Theologicis Disciplinis*, Bassani, 1742.

Blat, Albertus, O. P., *Commentarium Textus Codicis Juris Canonici, Liber III*, Romae, 1920.

Boringa, Antonius Maria, *Institutiones Theologico Dogmatico Canonico Historico Morales*, Venetiis, 1764.

Bouvier, J. B., *Institutiones Theologicae, Parisiis*, 1884.

Cappello, Felix M., S. J., *Tractatus Canonico-Moralis de Sacramentis*, Taurinorum Augustae, 1923.

Cappello, Felix M., S. J., *Institutiones Juris Publici Ecclesiastici*, Taurini, 1913.

Cappello, Felix M., S. J., *De Censuris juxta Codicem Juris Canonici*, Augustae Taurinorum, 1919.

Carbone, Caesar, *Praxis Ordinandorum*, Taurini, 1919.

Catalanus, Josephus, *Rituale Romanum Benedicti Papae XIV*, Patavii, 1760.

Catholic Encyclopedia, New York, 1907.

Cocaleo, P. Viatoris A., *Tentamina Theologico-Moralia,* Lucae, 1779.

Collectanea Sacrae Congregationis de Propaganda Fide, Romae, 1907.

Coronata, Matthaeus A., O. M. C., *De Locis et Temporibus Sacris,* Augustae Taurinorum, 1922.

Denziger, Henricus, *Enchiridion Symbolorum Definitionum et Declarationum de Rebus Fidei et Morum,* Friburgi, Brisgoviae, 1908.

De Augustinis, *De Re Sacramentaria,* Romae, 1889.

De Herdt, P. J. B., *Sacrae Liturgiae Praxis,* Lovanii, 1888.

Dictionnaire Encyclopédique de la Théologie Catholique, Paris, 1886.

Encyclopaedia of Religion and Ethics, Edited by James Hastings, New York, 1919.

Ferraris, F. Lucii, O. M. Reg. Obs. Sti. Francisci, *Bibliotheca Canonica, Juridica, Moralis, Theologica nec non Ascetica, Polemica, Rubricistica, Historica,* 9 *vols.,* Romae, 1892.

Genicot, Eduardus, S. J., *Institutiones Theologiae Moralis,* Bruxellis, 1922.

Hurter, H., S. J., *Theologiae Dogmaticae Compendium,* Oeniponte, 1889.

Katschthaler, Joannes, *Theologia Dogmatica Catholica Specialis,* Ratisbonae, 1884.

Kirchenlexikon, 12 *vols.,* Freiburg in Breisgau, 1901.

Kraus, F. X., *Real-Encyclopaedie der Christlichen Altherthuemer,* Freiburg in Breisgau, 1886.

Knoll, *Institutiones Theologiae Theoreticae,* Augustae Taurinorum, 1883.

Laymann, Paulus, S. J., *Theologiae Moralis,* Bambergae, 1669.

Lehmkuhl, Augustinus, S. J., *Theologia Moralis,* Friburgi, 1910.

Martene, Edmundus, *De Antiquis Ecclesiae Ritibus,* Rotomagi, 1700.

Moroto, Philippus, *Institutiones Juris Canonici ad Normam Novi Codicis*, Romae, 1921.

Noldin, H., S. J., *Summa Theologiae Moralis*, Oeniponte, 1922.

Pesch, Christianus, S. J., *Tractatus Dogmatici*, Friburgi, 1894.

Pohle-Preuss, *The Sacraments*, St. Louis, 1915.

Pontificale Romanum.

Pouratt, P., *La Théologie Sacramentaire*, Paris, 1910.

Probst, Ferdinand, *Sakramente und Sakramentalien in den drei ersten christlichen Jahrhunderten*, Tuebingen, 1872.

Probst, Ferdinand, *Liturgie der drei ersten christlichen Jahrhunderten*, Tuebingen, 1870.

Pruemmer, Dominicus M., O. P., *Manuale Theologiae Moralis secundum Principia S. Thomae Aq.*, Friburgi, Brisgoviae, 1923.

Plen. Conc. Baltimorensis II, 1866, Baltimore, 1868.

Ramsay, William, *A Manual of Roman Antiquities*, London, 1870.

Rituale Romanum.

Sabbetti-Barrett, *Compendium Theologiae Moralis*, Neo Eboraci, 1919.

S. Alphonsus Maria de Ligorio, *Theologia Moralis*, Torino, 1887.

S. Thomas Aq., *Summa*, Taurini, 1922.

Schmid, Fr., *Die Sakramentalien der Katholischen Kirche*, Muenchen, 1843.

Schulte, A. J., *Benedicenda*, New York, 1907.

Schulte, A. J., *Consecranda*, New York, 19

Smit, Johannes, *De Daemoniacis*, Romae, 1913.

Suarez, Franciscus, S. J., *Opera Omnia*, Parisiis, 1860.

Tanquerey, A., *Synopsis Theologiae Dogmaticae*, Romae, 1919.

Vermeersch-Creusen, *Epitome Juris Canonici, Cum Commentariis ad Scholas et ad Usum Privatum*, Mechliniae, 1921.

Wernz, Franciscus, S. J., *Jus Decretalium*, Romae, 1901.

Universitas Catholica Americae

Washingtonii, D. C.

Facultas Iuris Canonici

1924-1925

No. 28

DEUS LUX MEA

THESES

QUAS

AD DOCTORATUS GRADUM

IN

IURE CANONICO

Apud Universitatem Catholicam Americae

CONSEQUENDUM

PUBLICE PROPUGNABIT

JOANNES LINUS PASCHANG

SACERDOS DIOECESIS OMAHENSIS

IURIS CANONICI LICENTIATUS

HORA VIII A. M. DIE XIX MAII A. D. MCMXXV

I.	Canones	1-7.	De Ambitu Codicis.
II.	Canones	8-9.	De Promulgatione Legum Ecclesiasticarum.
III.	Canones	12-14.	De Legis Canonicae Subjecto.
IV.	Canones	80-86.	De Dispensationibus.
V.	Canones	91-95.	De Domicilio et Quasi-Domicilio.
VI.	Canones	97-98.	De Consanguinitate et Affinitate.
VII.	Canon	466.	De Missa pro Populo.
VIII.	Canones	738-744.	De Ministro Baptismi.
IX.	Canon	804.	De Admissione Sacerdotis Extranei.
X.	Canones	820-823.	De Tempore et Loco Missae Celebrandae.
XI.	Canones	845-852.	De Ministro Sacrae Communionis.
XII.	Canon	883.	De Iurisdictione Sacerdotis Iter Arripientis.
XIII.	Canones	1022-1026.	De Bannis.
XIV.	Canones	1144-1145.	De Notione Sacramentalium et de Potestate Ecclesiae in Eis.
XV.	Canones	1146-1150.	De Ministris et Ritibus Sacramentalium.
XVI.	Canones	1151-1153.	De Exercismo.
XVII.	Canones	1154-1160.	De Locis Sacris.
XVIII.	Canones	1170, 1172-1177.	De Violatione et Reconciliatione Ecclesiarum.
XIX.	Canones	1199-1200.	De Consecratione et Execratione Altaris.
XX.	Canones	1250-1254.	De Abstinentia et Ieiunio.

XXI. Canones 1594-1596. De Tribunali Ordinario Secundae Instantiae.
XXII. Canones 1598-1601. De Sacra Romana Rota.
XXIII. Canones 1750-1753. De Confessione Partium.
XXIV. Canones 1756-1758. Qui Testes esse Possint.
XXV. Canones 1789-1791. De Testimoniorum Fide.
XXVI. Canones 2195-2198. De Natura Delicti.
XXVII. Canon 2209. De Participatione in eodem Delicto.
XXVIII. Canones 2212-2213. De Conatu Delicti.
XXIX. Canones 2236-2240. De Poenarum Remissione.
XXX. Canones 2241-2244. De Natura Censurarum.
XXXI. Canon 2254. De Absolutione a Censura Reservata in Casibus Urgentioribus.
XXXII. Canones 2257-2259. De Notione Excommunicationis.
XXXIII. Canones 2350-2351. De Delictis Contra Vitam.

Ius Publicum

XXXIV. De Forma Regiminis in Ecclesia.
XXXV. De Iure Gladii.
XXXVI. De Iure Ecclesiae In Scholas.
XXXVII. De Iure Ecclesiae quoad Sacramentalia.
XXXVIII. De Iure Censurandi Libros.

Roman Law.

XXXIX. The Codex Juris Civilis—its Sources and Divisions.

XL. Enslavement—Modes and Effects of Enslavement.
XLI. Release from Slavery *ex lege* and its Effects.
XLII. Release from Slavery *ex manumissione* and its Effects.
XLIII. Colonus—His Legal Position, Duties and Rights.
XLIV. The Non-Cives.
XLV. Extinction and Suspension of Personality.
XLVI. Modification of Personality.
XLVII. Corporations.
XLVIII. Sponsalia.
XLIX. Matrimony—Concept, Form and Conditions.
L. Concubinatus in Roman Law.

INTERNATIONAL LAW

LI. Sources of International Law.
LII. Modes of Acquisition of Property.
LIII. Piracy.
LIV. Extradition.
LV. Monroe Doctrine.
LVI. Concordats.
LVII. Drago Doctrine.
LVIII. Jurisdiction over Vessels.
LIX. Protectorates, Suzerainties, Spheres of Influence and Mandates.
LX. Consuls.

* * * * * *

VIDIT SACRA FACULTAS:

PHILIPPUS BERNARDINI, S. T. D., J. U. D., Decanus.

H. LUDOVICUS MOTRY, S. T. D., J. C. D., p. t. a. Secretis.

VIDIT RECTOR UNIVERSITATIS:

THOMAS J. SHAHAN, S. T. D., J. U. L.

VITA.

John Linus Paschang was born October 5, 1895, at Hemingford, Nebraska. He received his elementary education in St. Anthony's Parochial School, at St. Charles, Nebraska, his secondary education at Conception College, Conception, Missouri. In September, 1916, he entered St. John's Seminary, Collegeville, Minnesota, and was ordained June 12, 1921. In the Fall of 1923 he entered the Catholic University of America and attended the lectures of Monsignor Dr. Philip Bernardini, Rev. Dr. Hubert L. Motry, Rev. Dr. Valentine T. Schaaf, O. S. F., Rev. Dr. Frances Lardone and Dr. Manoel de Oliveira Lima, to all of whom he hereby extends his sincerest thanks.

www.ingramcontent.com/pod-product-compliance
Lightning Source LLC
LaVergne TN
LVHW050207080826
844660LV00012B/371

* 9 7 8 0 8 1 3 2 2 2 1 8 9 *